TREASURES OF THE TRAIL

A Nature Guide to Edworthy Park,
Lawrey Gardens and the Douglas Fir Trail

The Edworthy Park Heritage Society
Edited by Jerry Osborn

This book is dedicated to all of the children – past, present and future – of Edworthy Park.

© Sean Jackson

TABLE OF CONTENTS

ACKNOWLEDGMENTS

The Edworthy Park Heritage Society gratefully acknowledges generous financial assistance from:

Calgary Community Lottery Board   Alberta Ecotrust   Calgary Field Naturalists' Society

We wish to thank the following individuals and organizations:

Dr. Wayne Lynch for his kind donation of 89 bird, mammal, reptile and amphibian photos;

Dr. O.F. Wachtler, Kathleen Roman, Michael Buckley, Paul Beaulieu, Sean Jackson, Dave Elphinstone, Gillean Daffern, Sonia Gonsalves, E. Gilliam, L. McConnell, M. Bailey, Urs Kallen, Bill Robinson, George Wilson, Lindsay Utting, and Anthony Heazell for generously donating photos;

Accumedia Technology Ltd. and Kallen Graphics Ltd. for supplying the electronic scans;

Kallen Graphics Ltd. for the layout, design, maps, production and printing;

Mel Buschert of Accumedia Technology Ltd. and Susan Otterson of ABL Imaging Ltd. for their helpful advice;

Tony Daffern of Rocky Mountain Books for donating the scans of G. Daffern's photos;

Dr. George Edworthy for permission to use the Edworthy family photos and graciously providing us with additional information about Edworthy Park;

Ron Linden for historical information about Lawrey Gardens;

Lynnette Wopnford and Michelle Theam for initial preparation of maps and diagrams;

Jeanette Motter for permission to print the painting, "Brickburn Deserted – 1936" by Douglas Motter;

Ed McCullough of Fedirchuk, McCullough and Associates (FMA) for archaeology advice and Allison Bailey, also of FMA, for designing the "Story in Stone";

Gus Yaki, Aileen Pelzer, Ted Pike, Len Hills and Reid Barclay for help with natural history content;

Les Adler for photographic access to his Paskapoo/Porcupine Hills fossil collection;

Graham Smith for sharing his knowledge about the park;

Faye Nicholson for typing;

Glenbow Museum (Archives) for permission to use historic photos and to quote archival materials;

John Acorn, C. Dana Bush, Dr. John Feltwell, Don Gayton, Jack Manson, Tom Willock, Calgary Field Naturalists' Society, Provincial Museum of Alberta (C.D. Bird et al.), Federation of Alberta Naturalists, Alpine Book Peddlers (George W. Scotter and Hälle Flygare), Greystone Books Douglas & McIntyre Publishing Group, Oxford University Press, McGraw-Hill Publishing Company, University of Calgary Press, City of Calgary Parks and Recreation and Engineering Departments, City of Calgary Archives, Calgary Herald, Lee Valley Tools Ltd. and Algrove Publishing, Alberta Community Development, Professor Michael C. Wilson, and Robert D.D. Cormack on behalf of the estate of R.G.H. Cormack for their kind permission to quote from their respective books and resources;

Nova Photo Centre, Mountain Equipment Co-op, Socrates' Corner, Dana Ashman Royal LePage Benchmark for sponsoring the Society's photo contest;

Gus Yaki, Nancy Shamanna, Andrea Gagnon, John Davey, Evelyn Osborn, and Kate Peach for proofreading and commenting on the text (any errors remain the Society's responsibility); and

The Board of Directors of the Edworthy Park Heritage Society for undertaking the logistics of producing and compiling a book.

INTRODUCTION

Umbrella-plants. Quarries. Eagles. Landslides. Tipi rings. Orchids. Homesteads. Buffalo jumps. Glacial erratics. River. Tortoise Shell butterflies. Fossilized giant lizards. Springs...

The semi-wild land south of the Bow River and north of Bow Trail is to some people the most interesting natural area in Calgary. The setting is a dramatic escarpment cut by the river and adjacent floodplain, in which much of the city's geologic history is revealed. A juxtaposition of prairie, forest and river creates diverse habitats for a great variety of plants and animals, including some of the easternmost Douglas-firs in Canada. Stamped on the landscape is a fascinating imprint of human history, involving native encampments and buffalo stampedes, ranches, market gardens and brick factories, flood damage and collapsing slopes. Fortunately for Calgarians, access to this land is provided by Edworthy Park, a regional pathway, and what is probably the most delightful walking trail in town, the Douglas Fir Trail and its satellite, Quarry Road Trail. This book is an interpretation of the area, designed to both introduce the district to neophytes, and expand the horizons of veteran visitors. The book begins with overview chapters summarizing the natural and human history of the area, and then takes the reader on five walking tours to illustrate that natural and human history.

As the City of Calgary grows rapidly, increased use creates pressures on the relatively small areas of Edworthy Park, Lawrey Gardens and the Douglas Fir Trail. Please join with us in preserving these unique natural areas. Simple acts such as carrying out litter, staying on trails, and leaving wildflowers, berries, trees (including deadwood), frogs, fossils, bison bones and other objects as found, will ensure the preservation of these natural areas for generations to come. Everything we have described may be seen from the trail.

We hope you learn as much as we have, and enjoy these natural areas as much as we do.

LEFT COLUMN Common Redpoll © Wayne Lynch Porcupine © Wayne Lynch Douglas Fir Trail © Lindsay Utting

CENTRE COLUMN Bald Eagle © Wayne Lynch Yellow Umbrella-plant © E. Gilliam Common Mergansers © Wayne Lynch Boreal Chorus Frog with vocal sac inflated © George Wilson

RIGHT COLUMN Round-leaved Orchid © Wayne Lynch Fossil Clams © E. Gilliam Richardson Ground Squirrel © Wayne Lynch

GEOLOGY AND PALAEONTOLOGY

By Jerry Osborn and Craig Scott

The most dramatic escarpment in Calgary is the slope rising from the south side of the Bow River in Edworthy Park and below the communities of Wildwood and Spruce Cliff. Indeed, there is no other slope in Calgary high and steep enough to earn the moniker "cliff". The escarpment displays the essential ingredients of the city's geologic story: bedrock, fossils, surficial sediments, groundwater, and river erosion. As a bonus, the slope illustrates the landslide hazards that characterize some reaches of the river's valley.

GEOLOGY

BEDROCK Calgary rests on an erosion surface commonly known as the "plains". Under the surface are sediments that eroded off the Cordilleran mountains that were rising to the west during the time of dinosaurs. The sediments underneath Calgary are thus tiny bits of mountain mass from British Columbia. The uppermost sediments, mostly grains of sand and particles of clay, were ultimately cemented and/or compacted into sandstone and shale, respectively, and are now referred to as the Porcupine Hills Formation. Geologists previously referred to this unit as the "Paskapoo Formation" which is the source of the former name of Canada Olympic Park. These rocks constitute the bedrock foundation of Calgary and are exposed in various parts of the escarpment, in and southeast of Edworthy Park. The Wildwood Slide scar is a good place to see the alternating layers of sandstone and shale.

The Porcupine Hills Formation is of Palaeocene age which is that period of time roughly 60 million years ago that immediately followed the demise of the dinosaurs. The sets of inclined layers ("cross-beds" in geological parlance) one sees in the sandstone outcrops are the type seen in modern river sediments, so the original sand is thought to have been deposited in a system of Palaeocene rivers that wandered back and forth across the plains of that time. The clay now represented by the shale component of the formation may have been deposited in back swamps along the ancient floodplains. At the time these rivers were running, the Canadian Rockies proper had not yet been built, because there are certain minerals in the Porcupine Hills sandstone that are endemic to British Columbia; these minerals could not have been carried to Alberta with a continental divide in the way.

LEFT *Spruce Cliff after a spring snowstorm. Wildwood Slide on left.* © J. Osborn

ABOVE *Cross-bedding in the Porcupine Hills sandstone in a quarry next to Quarry Road Trail. Inclined Layers above abut horizontal layers below.* © J. Osborn

The Porcupine Hills Formation was very significant in the early history of Calgary; it was the source of the sandstone blocks that were quarried to construct the downtown Calgary of the late 19th and early 20th centuries. There were probably many reasons leading to the eventual demise of sandstone construction. One reason was geological: the sandstone at and just below the ground surface was ultimately used, and the underlying unweathered sandstone proved very difficult to excavate.

SURFICIAL SEDIMENTS "Surficial Sediments" are sediments that have not yet transformed into rock, by virtue of their youth and lack of deep burial. An engineer would call such material "soil". In Calgary, most such sediments are a legacy of the Ice Age, but some pre-date and some post-date the glacial period.

There are no pre-glacial deposits on the Spruce Cliff escarpment itself, as the escarpment is a product of post-glacial, and possibly, glacial time. The flat top of Broadcast Hill, however, rising above Brickburn and Patterson Heights, is a small remnant of the pre-glacial landscape. Underneath a thin veneer of glacial sediment on the Broadcast Hill plateau are 10 to 15 m of river gravels. These gravels are

of the same thickness and composition, are at the same elevation, and gently slope in the same direction, as the river gravels on top of Nose Hill. The two hills therefore are thought to be the last remnants of a plains surface that existed in the Calgary area before the Bow Valley was cut. Fossil snails from the gravels on Nose Hill are roughly one million years old, which must be the age of the old river system flowing across what is now Broadcast Hill.[1] The bit of plain now called Broadcast Hill was isolated (and hence became a "hill") by downcutting of the Bow and Elbow rivers on the north, east, and south, and previously existing streams, possibly of glacial age, on the west. During this incision process the river paused for a bit (hundreds or thousands of years?) and cut the Wildwood bench by migrating laterally. The communities of Wildwood and Spruce Cliff rest on a layer of river gravel lying on this bench.

Most of the sedimentary record of the Ice Age along the escarpment has been removed by post-glacial erosion, but a story can be reconstructed from the well-preserved record across the river. There, a thick pile of glacial sediments partly fills the pre-glacial Bow Valley that was cut into the Porcupine Hills Formation. Varsity Acres, the University of Calgary campus, and Capitol Hill, for example, are built on the flat top of this fill. There are two basic kinds of glacial sediment here: glacial "till", which is deposited directly by or from glacier ice, and fine-grained glacial lake sediments. Glacier ice flowed in from both east (the "Laurentide Ice Sheet") and west (the "Bow Valley Glacier"), and coalesced in what is now central Calgary. A kilometre of ice covered the site. Once the Bow Valley ice began to retreat, meltwater from that ice was dammed by the Laurentide Ice Sheet, forming the glacial lake.

The glacial sediments, at the conclusion of glaciation, extended all the way across the valley, from the flank of Nose Hill to the flank of Broadcast Hill, as a continuous blanket. Re-incision of the Bow River in

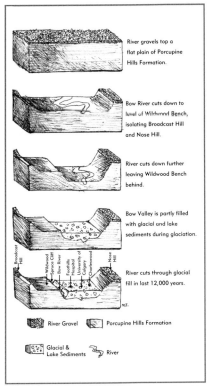

River gravels top a flat plain of Porcupine Hills Formation.

Bow River cuts down to level of Wildwood Bench, isolating Broadcast Hill and Nose Hill.

River cuts down further leaving Wildwood Bench behind.

Bow Valley is partly filled with glacial and lake sediments during glaciation.

River cuts through glacial fill in last 12,000 years.

River Gravel | Porcupine Hills Formation

Glacial & Lake Sediments | River

FIGURE 1 *Evolution of central Calgary landscape. Sketch by Michelle Theam*

postglacial time removed the strip of that blanket that was adjacent to Spruce Cliff and Edworthy Park, hence, most of the glacial sediment east of Sarcee Trail is gone. The bedrock slope of Spruce Cliff is mantled with a veneer of surficial sediment up to several metres thick, some of which appears to be till, but most has been reworked by gravity-driven downslope movement, and, as such, is referred to as "colluvium".

At the very top of the Wildwood Slide scar can be seen several metres' thickness of gravel overlying the Porcupine Hills bedrock. This gravel extends back from the crest of the escarpment and underlies the communities of Wildwood and Spruce Cliff. It appears to be a chaotic form of river gravel, and probably was deposited by glacial meltwater streams during glaciation.

Modern (post-glacial) Bow River deposits occur at the base of the escarpment (e.g., underneath the CPR tracks) and underneath Lawrey Gardens, and form the lower level of Edworthy Park. There are no data on ages of the river deposits in Edworthy Park, but similar deposits across the river at Point McKay were deposited over the last 4,000 years.[2] East of Crowchild Trail, the post-glacial river gravels widen out to form the extensive bench that underlies downtown Calgary.

The most prominent physiographic feature in Edworthy Park is the great coulee, referred to in this book as "the Coulee", which cuts through the escarpment and provides vehicle access to the picnic areas on the floodplain. About 600 m long and 45 m deep at its mouth, it drains part of the northeastern flank of Broadcast Hill. The Coulee hosts the occasional raging torrent during a storm but most of the time it is dry. That, and the rather small drainage area upstream, renders the origin of the Coulee a bit problematic: there seems to have been a lot of erosion caused by little running water. It is conceivable that the Coulee held a permanent spring-fed stream prior to urban development; on the other hand, perhaps intermittent storm-producing floods were enough to do the job.

Most of the sediment created by erosion of the Coulee has gone down the Bow River but some of it remains in a small "alluvial fan" between the Coulee mouth and the CPR tracks (and underlying the parking lot). "Alluvium" is sediment deposited out of a river or stream, and "fan" describes the shape of a sediment body often built up at the mouth of a canyon or coulee.

GROUNDWATER To most people groundwater is out of sight and out of mind, but its existence is obvious along the Spruce Cliff/Edworthy Park escarpment, where the water discharges from the ground in dozens of springs. The source of the water is rainfall that infiltrates the ground surface on the top and flanks of Broadcast Hill and on the lower ground east of Sarcee Trail. Some of the percolating water ends up in the gravels overlying the bedrock and flows sideways through the gravel, eventually emanating in the escarpment as "contact springs" at the boundary between gravel and bedrock. Some of the infiltrating water penetrates the bedrock, probably through fractures in the rock, and ends up in sandstone beds. The water travels sideways through the sandstone and produces springs in the escarpment. An excellent example of these bedrock springs is the prominent spring in the Wildwood Slide scar: groundwater can be seen seeping or trickling out where sandstone overlies shale in the upper part of the scar, a bit left of centre. When winter ends and snow melts on the scar, the frozen waterfall below the spring becomes obvious. The two most prominent springs in Edworthy Park are also bedrock springs.

The springwater running down parts of Spruce Cliff is responsible for some perpetual headaches in the Engineering Department at City Hall. Water renders the surficial sediment more unstable, and contributes both to slumping of discrete masses of sediment, and slow, gradual downhill creep of sediment all over the slope. Furthermore, the water running down from springs freezes in winter to form

TOP *Wildwood Slide. The grassy lower half of the slope is slumped debris derived from the upper half of the slope.* © J. Osborn

BOTTOM *Bench destroyed (1999) by falling sandstone boulder, on the regional pathway on the south side of the Bow River.* © J. Osborn

"icings", and the ice builds up on the bike path below as well as on the slope. A common springtime sight at the base of the escarpment is early-season bicyclists hauling their bikes up and over the mini-glaciers with one hand while desperately gripping the chain-link fence with the other hand. The City has attempted to manage the water by constructing vertical drains below major springs; these drains connect to pipes that extend underneath the CPR tracks to the river but the drainage system is not overly successful.

SLOPE INSTABILITY As befitting a slope that is relatively high and steep, Spruce Cliff experiences gravity-driven downslope movement of rock and soil, a process known as "mass movement" or "mass wasting". Gradual, imperceptible downslope motion of soil is termed "creep", while the terms "slump" and "landslide" are applied to failing bodies of rock/soil with discrete failure surfaces. "Flows" usually contain water and move as semi-liquids. All these have occurred on the escarpment.

The most obvious case is the relatively bare swath of the so-called Wildwood Slide. No one seems to know when or exactly how the slide first happened, but in the middle decades of the 20th century, a hummocky mass of debris that had moved down from the bedrock scar lay upslope of the CPR tracks, and occasionally would creep over the tracks or yield debris flows that covered the tracks. The springs discharging at the site are a major cause of this instability; Calgary engineers believe that some of the seepage was consequent to a rise in groundwater elevation that followed development of the Wildwood and Spruce Cliff communities in the 1950s. The City initiated a remediation effort in the 1970s: drainage pipes were installed in the subsurface to collect ground and surface water and run it under the tracks, and the hummocky slide mass was graded and landscaped to create the grassed slope visible today.

Several other zones of instability exist on the escarpment; these are generally masses of surficial sediment that are slumping at creep (i.e., imperceptible) rates, usually assisted by springwater. In addition, small debris flows occasionally run across the bike path in spring when snow and spring icings are melting. Rockfall is not considered a problem in Calgary, but a large sandstone boulder bounced down the escarpment in 1999 and destroyed a bench on the bike path; hopefully no one was sitting there at the time.

PALAEONTOLOGY

Palaeontology in Alberta has enjoyed a long and rich history, dating back to the late 1800s. Fossils from Alberta have been known for nearly 100 years and have figured significantly in the understanding of local and regional geology, stratigraphy, and the evolutionary history of plants, dinosaurs, and mammals. Outcrops in the City of Calgary have played an important role in palaeontological research in Alberta, as there are numerous fossil-bearing sites located along the banks of rivers and streams in the city, and at isolated outcrops, including those at Edworthy Park. The reasons are that (1) the ancient river environments in which the Porcupine Hills Formation was deposited, and the climate of the time, were ideal for the transportation, deposition, and subsequent fossilization of organic remains, and (2) downcutting of the modern rivers and streams in Calgary has exposed the rock in cross-section. Hence the formation has yielded abundant assemblages of fossilized plants and animals in Calgary and throughout most of south-central Alberta.

During Palaeocene time the climate had begun to shift from the warm, tropical conditions in which the dinosaurs flourished to a subtropical and eventually to a temperate system. Mammals, although present throughout the reign of the dinosaurs, began to rapidly diversify and establish themselves as the dominant terrestrial organisms, and shared the landscape with fish, amphibians, reptiles, and birds. Plants rapidly diversified, with angiosperms, or flowering plants, becoming increasingly abundant and effectively taking over from the conifer-dominated landscape of the Mesozoic. The fossils from Edworthy Park and vicinity reflect this diversity of organisms, and the following provides an overview of some of the more important fossils discovered.

PLANTS Leaf impressions were the first discovered fossils from Edworthy Park, and are common throughout the Porcupine Hills Formation in Alberta. Both gymnosperms (coniferous plants) and angiosperms (flowering plants) are represented in Porcupine Hills strata, although only angiosperm fossils are currently known from Edworthy Park, among which are fossilized forms similar to those living today. *Pterospermites* (Family Sterculiaceae), represented by fairly large fossils, is in the family that includes modern forms such as the Buddha's Coconut, Looking-glass Plant, and Skunk Tree. Interestingly, this family of plants contains members that today produce chocolate, cocoa and cola nuts. *Platanus* (Family Platanaceae) is represented by large fossilized leaves, some up to 30 cm in length. This group of plants, commonly called the Sycamore Family, is widely distributed today, and abundantly represented in North America. Two other important groups of plants are represented at Edworthy Park, *Betula* (Family Betulaceae; birches) and *Populus* (Family Salicaceae; poplars, willows). Today, these plants are important in the timber industry and as pioneer species in the re-establishment of stands after burns. In addition, a spectacular diversity of fossil plants can be found elsewhere in Porcupine Hills strata, particularly in the Red Deer River valley. Of these, some of the more interesting groups include ginkgos (Family Ginkgoaceae), horsetails (Family Equisetaceae), deciduous evergreens (Family Taxodiaceae), and mosses (Family Ricciaceae). Fossil plants generally occur in fine to medium grained sandstones, and are frequently represented by leaves, leaf impressions, stems, and more rarely, seedlings and cones.

MOLLUSCS Freshwater molluscs are a common constituent of river deposits; their hard parts preserve readily, and these invertebrates are often the most abundantly represented fossils in any given layer. In Edworthy Park, the spiral shells of gastropods (snails) and flat shells of bivalves (clams) are very well preserved, often intact and three-dimensional, suggesting that they may have lived in gently flowing streams. They generally occur in dark shales and fine-grained siltstones. Fossil molluscs are ubiquitous throughout the Porcupine Hills Formation in Alberta, and, where well represented, can be used in dating rocks.

FISH Organic material is usually transported by rivers and streams prior to burial, so it is not surprising that fish comprise a large portion of any given fossil assemblage. Fish are among the best-represented groups in the Porcupine Hills Formation, occurring almost as a rule in freshwater deposits. Among the fossils collected at Edworthy Park, Amia (Order Amiiformes; bowfin) and Lepisosteus (Order Lepisosteiformes; gar) are common, represented by bones, scales, and teeth, only rarely preserved as complete specimens. Both forms are predaceous and likely preyed on invertebrates or other, smaller fish. These groups of fish are still with us today and are considered by many to be "living fossils".

AMPHIBIANS AND REPTILES Amphibians and reptiles are relatively common in the Porcupine Hills Formation, and are indicators of semi-aquatic environments. Among the most abundant are the albanerpetontids (Order Allocaudata, distant relatives of modern salamanders), crocodilians (Order Crocodyliformes, relatives of modern crocodiles and alligators), and a variety of tiny lizards. Of particular interest, numerous bones of a large lizard, Champsosaurus, (Order Choristodera) have been collected from Edworthy Park. Champsosaurs were semi-aquatic reptiles that appear superficially crocodile-like, with a long, pointed snout, armed with sharp teeth. These creatures are presumed to have led a crocodile-like existence, and were probably one of the top carnivores of the day; they became extinct at the end of the Palaeocene, leaving no successors. Although not represented in the Edworthy Park collection, fossil turtles are also common constituents of Porcupine Hills rock. Fish, amphibians, and reptiles occur in dark shales and in fine-grained silt and sandstones, ideal for the preservation of their small bones and teeth.

MAMMALS Mammals comprise a small portion of the Edworthy Park collection, but are relatively common and important constituents of Porcupine Hills rock. As with the amphibians and reptiles, mammalian remains are usually restricted to small bones and teeth, and occur in dark shales and siltstones. Most of the mammals from the Porcupine Hills Formation, and all discovered at Edworthy Park, were small, shrew-like creatures, many of which were the precursors to the modern orders of mammals. Of particular interest were the multituberculates (Order Multituberculata), a group of unusual, rodent-like mammals that were common in Mesozoic and Palaeocene times. These creatures are characterized by strange, blade-like teeth with many cusps, and are presumed to have been herbivorous and arboreal, likely eating fruit and foliage high atop the trees of the subtropical Palaeocene forests, much in the way modern squirrels do today. Another interesting diminutive mammal, Paromomys (Order Primates), is well represented at Edworthy Park. This creature, also presumed to have led an arboreal existence, is a distant relative of modern flying lemurs of southeast Asia, and perhaps glided between branches in search of its next meal. Included among the diverse mammals from the Palaeocene of Alberta were primitive ungulates, the ancestors of such modern groups as horses, rhinoceroses, cows, deer, and bison; marsupials that possibly gave rise to modern opossums; and tiny insectivorous creatures distantly related to modern hedgehogs and shrews. In their totality, mammals are undoubtedly the best represented animals from the Palaeocene of Alberta and comprise one of the most complete fossil records of all known organisms. Because of their exquisite record, fossil mammals are used extensively in the dating of terrestrial sediments in North America.

Despite the successful palaeontological activities in Calgary and area, much work is yet to be done. We have only scratched the surface of what is surely an important geographical and geological area in the study of early Cenozoic life, and our understanding of the dynamic Palaeocene ecosystem is just beginning. Undoubtedly, sites in and around Calgary will be pivotal in reconstructing past life, and understanding the organisms that inhabited this region some 60 million years ago.

TOP RIGHT Ginkgoites adiantoides (Les Adler Collection) © Michael Buckley

BOTTOM LEFT Cercidiphyllum articum (Les Adler Collection) © Michael Buckley

BOTTOM RIGHT Metasequoia occidentalis (Les Adler Collection) © Michael Buckley

Footnotes – Geology and Palaeontology

[1]   G. Osborn, R. Thomas, W. McCoy, B. Miller and Smith, "Significance of a molluscan fauna to the physiographic history of the Calgary area, Alberta", *Canadian Journal of Earth Sciences* 28: pp. 1948-1955.

[2]   Michael C. Wilson, *Once Upon a River: Archaeology and Geology of the Bow River Valley at Calgary, Alberta, Canada*, Archaeological Survey of Canada, Paper No. 114, National Museum of Man Mercury Series.

PLANT LIFE

By Gustave J. Yaki

In the "Calgary's Natural Areas" report on the plants of Edworthy Park, published by the Calgary Field Naturalists' Society's Natural Areas Committee in December 1980, it was stated that there were 59 fungi and slime molds, 30 lichens, 3 liverworts, 53 mosses and 335 vascular plant species present.

The fungi are no longer considered to be plants and are now in a separate kingdom more closely allied to animals. Lichens, too, are a unique group. They are composed of two species – one a fungus, the other an alga – forming a symbiotic partnership: both can live independently but benefit by living together. The mosses and liverworts are true plants, in a group called Bryophytes. They transport water and nutrients from cell to cell by osmosis. As a result, they seldom grow to any size, usually under six centimetres high.

The remaining group, the vascular plants, totalled 335 species in the 1980 report. In 2001, an additional 50 species were found. If all the original species were correctly identified and are still present, the list now exceeds 380 species. Additional species are still likely to be found.

Undoubtedly, since the arrival of Europeans, both the diversity of native species and abundance of flowering plants have been greatly altered within the park area. The historical human activity, especially cultivation and the grazing of livestock, has had an impact that is hard to measure. One can only contemplate what species were once present that are gone now. (Actually, because pollen grains endure seemingly forever, it would be possible, but time-consuming, to reconstruct earlier plant assemblages).

The vascular plants comprise those species most of us call to mind when the word "plant" is mentioned. They have internal capillary-like tubes that permit the transfer of moisture and nutrients to all parts of the plant, regardless of size, even to the top of the tallest living organism (e.g., the Coast Redwoods of California, over 115 metres high). Out of the 380 species in the park at least 100 are non-native. They were introduced accidentally or intentionally. Most were carried by the wind or water or animals. Some arrived as seeds dropped from boxcars as trains passed through the park. Some may have dropped from your clothes as you hiked the trails. For the most part, these introduced plants have left their diseases, parasites and predators behind. As a result, once established, most quickly increased their number, thus out-competing the original species. Sadly, unless controlled, this probably will

LEFT *Rushes, Lawrey Gardens* © O.F. Wachtler

result in the disappearance of many more native species in future years.

Edworthy Park contains about 20 species of vascular plants which are seldom or never noted elsewhere within the city of Calgary. Some of the more noteworthy species, listed in phylogenetic order, are:

Douglas-fir (*Pseudotsuga menziesii*), Slender Arrow-Grass (*Triglochin palustris*), Switchgrass (*Panicum virgatum*), False Solomon's-seal (*Smilacina racemosa*), Dwarf False Asphodel (*T. pusilla*), Pale Blue-eyed Grass (*Sisyrinchium septentrionale*), Sparrow's-egg or Franklin Lady's-slipper Orchids (*Cypripedium passerinum*), Paper Birch (*Betula papyrifera*), Small Wood Anemone (*Anemone parviflora*), Creeping Spearwort (*Ranunculus reptans*), Tall Meadow Rue (*Thalictrum dasycarpum*), White Meadowsweet (*Spiraea betulifolia*), Bog Violet (*Viola nephrophylla*), Saline Shooting Star (*Dodecatheon pulchellum*), Wild Sarsaparilla (*Aralia nudicaulis*), Mealy Primrose (*Primula incana*), Eyebright (*Euphrasia arctica*) and Common Butterwort (*Pinguicula vulgaris*). In 1980, Blue Flag (*Iris missouriensis*), a rare Alberta species, was listed as occurring in a rubble dump. It has not knowingly been seen lately. Twisted-stalk (*Streptopus amplexifolius*), with only one plant noted in 1980, and other native species may already be gone. River Alder (*Alnus tenufolia*) was listed in 1980 but not found in 2001. This is a long-lived species, so hopefully it was just missed and is still there.

Because of their rarity, all native plants, particularly those of the above species, deserve to be better protected. Unfortunately, certain people (such as some mountain-bikers riding off trails, who do appreciate having access to the natural landscape but who have not yet developed an understanding of their relationship with the natural world) are threatening their future existence.

The flagship plant of Edworthy Park undoubtedly is the Douglas-fir tree, first collected by the young Scottish botanist David Douglas in the early 1800s. It is the dominant species along the upper half of the north-facing slope and, of course, the namesake of the Douglas Fir Trail. While never nearing the size of its counterparts west of the continental divide, some reach a diameter of a half metre or more and are 300-500 years of age. It is a conifer recognized by the deep-fissured bark on mature trees and the flat needle-like leaves. The striking diagnostic feature is the bracts (or "mouse-tails") sticking out from under the cone scales.

The most primitive of the vascular plants, the spore-producing plants or Pteridophytes, are the ferns and their allies, represented in the park by one club-moss (Little Club-Moss, or *Selaginella densa*), six species of horsetails or scouring rushes (*Equisetum spp.*), and one fern – Fragile Fern (*Cystopteris fragilis*).

The seed-producing plants, the Spermatophytes, are divided into two groups. The first, the Gymnosperms, which usually produce seeds under scales, are represented by six species of conifers: two junipers (*Juniperus spp.*), the Douglas-fir and two spruces. White Spruce (*Picea glauca*) is the most common tree in the park while Blue Spruce (*P. pungens*) and Japanese Larch (*Larix japonica*) have been planted as ornamentals.

Within the second group, the Angiosperms, whose seeds are usually in a protective

ABOVE *Bulrush, South Sora Pond* © E. Gilliam

cover, there are also two further divisions. Those with one seed-leaf (known as a cotyledon) upon germination, the Monocotyledons, contain at least ten families found in the park. Typically they have parallel-veined leaves and flower parts in threes or multiples of three.

Of these, Wide-leaved Cat-tail (*Typha latifolia*), two species of pondweeds (*Potomogeton spp.*) and Arrowhead (*Sagittaria cuneata*) are aquatics present in ponds or the river. Some forty species of grasses and at least eight sedges also occur. Most notable of the grasses is Switchgrass (*Panicum virgatum*), growing on the north side of the railway about 400 m east of the Harry Boothman Bridge (a pedestrian bridge). This is an eastern tall-grass prairie species.

At least three of the grass-like rushes (*Juncus spp.*) occur in moist, sunny locations. Allied to them are the lilies, represented by about a dozen types. That family contains the diminutive Dwarf False Asphodel of which only one specimen was noted in 2001.

The Orchids, which may be the world's largest plant family and which many think of as tropical, are represented by at least seven species. The most abundant is the Sparrow's-egg or Franklin's Lady's-slipper. At least 1,000 individual plants were noted in 2001. The others are Spotted Coralroot (*Corallorhiza maculata*), Striped Coralroot (*C. striata*), Early or Pale Coralroot, (*C. trifida*), Northern Green Orchid (*Platanthera hyperborea*), Bracted Green Orchid (*P. viridis*) and Round-leaved Orchis (*Orchis rotundifolia*).

The great bulk of plant species produce two seed-leaves or cotyledons upon germinating, thus are known as Dicotyledons. They are characterized by having net-veined leaves and generally have flower parts in fours or fives, or multiples thereof. They include all the remaining vascular plants, represented by about 37 families in the park.

RIGHT *Northern Green Orchid* © O.F. Wachtler

Leading the list of that group are families whose flowers are often inconspicuous (no showy petals) and usually pollinated by wind. Many blossom early, before insects are abundant. Included are the Willow/Poplar, Birch, Nettle, Knotweed, Goosefoot and Amaranth Families, to name a few.

The remaining plant families, containing the vast majority of species, usually have showy petals and/or sepals, making their flowers more noticeable. They generally bloom later in the season when insects are more abundant.

Learning to identify the plants adds enjoyment to your outing. Unfortunately, it requires several books to cover all the species found in Edworthy Park and vicinity. Some useful titles are listed in the Further Reading section. If book learning is not your style, you may want to join a group that goes afield to see the plants firsthand. The Calgary Field Naturalists' Society (CFNS) conducts free outings, including visits to Edworthy Park. You may obtain details of these outings by calling CFNS or checking the website. A plant checklist for the area is found in Appendix I.

LEFT *Groundsel* © O.F. Wachtler

TOP *Sticky Purple Geranium, may be seen next to Bow River Pathway* © O.F. Wachtler

MIDDLE *Heart-leaved Alexander* © O.F. Wachtler

BOTTOM *Red Baneberry, poisonous* © O.F. Wachtler

ANIMAL LIFE

By Gustave J. Yaki

Although Edworthy Park is quite near the centre of the city, it supports a great diversity of animal life mainly because of its location on the south bank of the Bow River, and its many habitat types. One can potentially still find approximately 25 mammal species, 150 bird, 2 reptile, 3 amphibian, 12 fish and innumerable invertebrate species.

Before the coming of Europeans, the diversity was even greater. Gone are the Plains Grizzly and Grey Wolf, and the Bison herds that they followed. Some of the smaller carnivores such as Wolverine, Fisher and Pine Marten are missing as well.

The variety of bird species probably hasn't changed as much. Some species, however, may have increased in numbers while sadly the majority have declined. Reptiles' numbers are reduced, as are those of amphibians. In fact, the Leopard Frog, abundant until the 1970s, is now totally extirpated. Its disappearance likely is due not only to local changes but seems linked to unknown and possibly global causes. Fish diversity may be greater today with the introduction of Brown and Rainbow Trout, but this is offset by the near total loss of Bull and Cutthroat Trout.

The invertebrate life has likely changed but no one knows to what degree. Because of alteration to the native vegetation, the diversity of insects and other arthropods which feed on these plants (and their predators) have likely declined. Moreover, the accidental or deliberate introduction of other arthropods, which have left their parasites, predators and diseases behind, has displaced many native species.

So what can one expect to see in the Edworthy Park area today?

MAMMALS Many of our mammal species lead nocturnal lives so they are not often seen. They, do, however, leave signs of their presence in the form of tracks, browsing, and scats. From this evidence one can infer their existence.

Some larger mammals such as Moose, Cougar, Canada Lynx, Striped Skunk, Black Bear, Red Fox, and American Badger that formerly visited, may on occasion follow the Bow River corridor and find themselves in the park. In the past, their presence would have been routine.

Mule Deer and White-tailed Deer are now resident. Coyotes are routinely seen: twenty-five years ago they were quite rare. With the disappearance of

LEFT *Least Chipmunk* © *Wayne Lynch*

the Wolf, Coyotes increased as they expanded their range, filling all possible niches. Long-tailed Weasel and possibly Least Weasel and Mink probably also occur from time to time. Beaver and Muskrat can be found in or along the Bow River. Porcupines still are present. The Least Chipmunk is now present, apparently so only in the past five years. A Red Squirrel can be heard chattering on almost every visit and with patience can be glimpsed. The introduced Gray Squirrel, in its varied grey or black morphs, can also sometimes be seen, especially in the picnic areas. It is possible that the Northern Flying Squirrel may be present, but as it is totally nocturnal, it is seldom observed. The Richardson's Ground Squirrel, popularly known as gopher, occurs on the short grass areas above the escarpment, especially on the western end of the park. The true gopher, the Northern Pocket Gopher, which lives a subterranean life, is the one responsible for the mounds of black soil in the park's grassy areas. The mounds are often incorrectly called mole hills. There are no moles in Alberta. Meadow Vole, Red-backed Vole, Deer Mouse and possibly other small rodents are present although seldom seen. In wooded areas, a careful observer will see Snowshoe Hare. On the grassy meadows above the escarpment, you may find White-tailed Jackrabbits. Several species of bats are observed from time to time. A Red Bat, rare in Calgary, was found here about four years ago but other species can be seen, particularly in migration during August. Finally, at least three species of shrews, amongst the smallest of mammals, are a possibility. Not known to occur, but expected soon, is the Raccoon. Raccoons entered the Canadian prairies fifty years ago and have been recorded in the Calgary area in recent years.

LEFT *Deer Mouse* © Wayne Lynch

TOP *Snowshoe Hare in winter* © Wayne Lynch

MIDDLE *Snowshoe Hare in spring* © E. Gilliam

BOTTOM *White-tailed Jackrabbit* © Wayne Lynch

ABOVE *Sharp-shinned Hawk* © Wayne Lynch

BIRDS Birds, except some owls and nightjars, are active during daylight hours; therefore they are more readily observed than most mammals. During the course of a year, one can usually see over 100 species. People familiar with birds routinely see fifty or more species during any summer outing; even in mid-winter a dozen or more kinds may be found.

At any time, there is a diversity of waterfowl on the open waters of the Bow River. About a dozen kinds of ducks, geese and swans, and sometimes Double-crested Cormorant and American White Pelican occur. Fifty years ago Canada Geese were rare, observed only during spring and autumn migration to and from their Arctic nesting grounds. About that time it was realized that a giant race of Canada Geese had formerly once bred in mid-continent. These were all but eliminated by early settlers in their march westward. Fortunately, a few were kept in captivity by hobbyists. It is from that remnant stock that all the Canada Geese that now nest and winter in Calgary originated. The duck species most likely to be identified throughout the year are Mallard, Common Goldeneye and Common Merganser.

Several kinds of hawks can be observed.

Red-tailed and Swainson's Hawks nest annually, as do American Kestrels and possibly Merlins. Northern Harriers are usually noted during migration and Northern Goshawks, Sharp-shinned and Cooper's Hawks are often seen in migration or in the winter months. Ospreys fish the Bow River from April to September while Bald Eagles are usually present during the colder times of the year.

Sharp-tailed Grouse no longer dance on the grassy uplands, but the introduced Gray Partridge, commonly called Hungarian Partridge because of where the source stock originated, is present in variable numbers year-round.

Sora (rails) and several shorebird species can be seen in or on wet areas during the summer or during the migration season. The most likely species are Killdeer, Spotted Sandpiper and Greater Yellowlegs, and sometimes Solitary Sandpiper. Ring-billed Gulls frequenting the river's islands from March to November, sometimes are joined by Franklin's, California and Herring Gulls. Other gull species visit Calgary from time to time. It is possible that one of them might fly along the Bow River and be noted by sharp-eyed observers. Rock Dove, the introduced feral pigeon, can always be seen, often feeding on grain spilled along the railway. The native Mourning Dove is a scarce summer visitor. A species new to North America, the Eurasian Collared-Dove, may have been observed in the park area on 17 July 2001. The species was probably self-introduced into Florida from the Bahamas in the 1980s and has rapidly spread across the continent. It is now resident in adjoining Saskatchewan and Montana.

Several owl species are regular. The Great Horned Owl and probably the diminutive Northern Saw-whet Owl nest annually. A Barred Owl was found on the east end of the Douglas Fir Trail on 26 March 2000. Formerly this was an eastern North American species but perhaps because timber cutting has created openings in the Aspen Parkland and/or Boreal Forest, it has moved westward. Also semi-nocturnal, the Common Nighthawk, our only nightjar, used to feed on flying insects high above the park on summer nights. Formerly it was a fairly common summer resident but has suffered drastic population declines. Speculation as to the cause often includes the high use of pesticide in the urban environment.

The Rufous Hummingbird is an uncommon summer resident. Two other hummingbird species that regularly visit the Calgary area – the Calliope and Ruby-throated Hummingbirds – may already be similar residents.

The Belted Kingfisher, with its big bushy crest, is an annual visitor, possible to see at any time of the year when there is open water along the Bow River. Northern Flickers and Downy and Hairy Woodpeckers are also to be expected year-round. Yellow-bellied Sapsuckers may be seen during the migration season while Pileated, Three-toed and Black-backed Woodpeckers are rarer possibilities most likely during the winter months.

The song-birds or Passerines, the largest order of birds, are represented by many species that visit the park. The Tyrant

TOP Blue Jays are now common ©Wayne Lynch

BOTTOM Gray Catbird may be seen on Lawrey Gardens. © Wayne Lynch

Flycatcher group contains such summer residents as Western Wood-Pewee, Least Flycatcher and Eastern Kingbird and regular migrants such as Olive-sided Flycatcher and Eastern Phoebe. Say's Phoebe and some of the smaller *Empidonax* flycatchers may occur from time to time.

Bank and Northern Rough-winged Swallows nest in holes on the vertical banks of the river while Cliff Swallows nest under the Boothman

TOP *Yellow-rumped Warbler* © Wayne Lynch
BOTTOM *Wilson's Warbler* © Wayne Lynch

TOP *Rose-breasted Grosbeak* © Wayne Lynch
BOTTOM *Chestnut-sided Warbler* © Wayne Lynch

Bridge. Tree Swallows use tree cavities in the Lawrey Gardens area. Barn Swallows also can be seen over the river from time to time. It is possible that Violet-green Swallows occasionally occur during migration.

The Northern Shrike, that unique songbird which preys on small rodents and birds as well as spiders and insects, occurs singly from October to April. Four members of the Vireo Family have been recorded: Red-eyed and Warbling as summer residents and Blue-headed and Philadelphia as migrants. The Crow Family is represented by the Blue Jay and Black-billed Magpie as year-round residents. The American Crow is present in summer, rarely in winter. Common Ravens can often be seen overhead, especially during the winter season. A very rare winter visitor is Clark's Nutcracker. The Gray Jay is another rare possibility during the cooler months, as is Steller's Jay.

Black-capped Chickadees are year-round residents. Two other chickadees, Boreal and Mountain, occasionally occur, usually during winter. Flocking with the chickadees sometimes are the nuthatches: Red-breasted in the coniferous woods and White-breasted (only in recent years) in the deciduous trees near the river. Often associated with the above group during October to March are Brown Creepers, mouse-like birds that creep high up the tree trunk only to fly down to the base of a nearby tree and repeat the process. Also in the coniferous stands one can find two of our tiniest birds (next in size only to hummingbirds): in summer, Ruby-crowned Kinglets and, in winter, Golden-crowned Kinglets.

American Robin and Veery breed in the park while at other seasons one might see a Hermit, Swainson's and/or Varied Thrush. Robins and the Varied Thrush may also be seen here during the winter months. Two other family members, Mountain Bluebird and Townsend's Solitaire, may occur during migration. The House Wren is an uncommon summer resident while the Winter Wren is present only during migration, particularly in the coniferous forest. The American Dipper, a songbird that walks under water to find its food, is a possibility in some winters. In summer the Gray Catbird is a regular nester in the taller shrubs at low elevations. The related Brown Thrasher has also nested in the park in the past.

The sleek-looking Cedar Waxwings regularly nest in the riverine forests and in some years a few try to survive our winters. During the colder months, from October to April, large flocks (up to 1,000 or more individuals) of Bohemian Waxwings may be encountered when heavy snows drive them from the bearberry slopes in the mountains.

The introduced European Starling nests in the poplar forest in cavities made by flickers and other woodpeckers. Some may be present on sunny days in the wintertime. Another introduced species, the House Sparrow, can frequently be found throughout the year.

Of our colourful wood-warblers, the Yellow Warbler and Common Yellowthroat both nest here; about a dozen other species may appear, particularly in the spring and more commonly during the autumn migration. Those most likely to be encountered are: Tennessee, Orange-crowned, Yellow-rumped, Blackpoll, Bay-breasted, Cape May, Black-and-White, Wilson's, MacGillivray's and Mourning Warbler and American Redstart.

The Tanager family is represented by one species, the brilliantly coloured Western, which is seen during migration in May and occasionally in August. It is possible that they nest in low numbers in the coniferous forest of Douglas-fir and White Spruce on the north-facing slopes. One sight record of a Scarlet Tanager is known.

A number of seed-eating finches and their allies occur. Among the summer residents expect Chipping, Clay-coloured, Savannah and Song Sparrow and rarely Dark-eyed Junco, one of which was seen in July 2001. During migration, watch for White-throated and White-crowned Sparrow and the secretive

TOP Evening Grosbeak (male) © Wayne Lynch
BOTTOM Dark-eyed Junco © Wayne Lynch

TOP Fox Sparrow © Wayne Lynch

BOTTOM White-crowned Sparrow © Wayne Lynch

TOP Savannah Sparrow © Wayne Lynch

BOTTOM American Tree Sparrow © Wayne Lynch

Lincoln's. In winter, you may find American Tree Sparrow along with more juncos.

Pine Grosbeak, Common Redpoll and Pine Siskin all occur, usually in winter. Purple Finch, Red Crossbill and White-winged Crossbill are also winter visitors but since they tend to follow the conifer cone crops, might be seen at almost any time of the year. The American Goldfinch is usually present in the summer months, but some stayed in Calgary during the 2001-2002 winter in small numbers. Evening Grosbeak, abundant during the winter months until the 1970s, now seldom appear, for reasons not clearly understood

The Blackbird or Icterid Family is represented by Red-winged Blackbird and Baltimore Oriole, both nesting here. For nest construction orioles sometimes use monofilament line discarded by careless fishermen. Unfortunately, adults or young can become entangled, resulting in their death, as observed at one nest in 2001. Other species in this family include Brewer's

Blackbird, Common Grackle and Brown-headed Cowbird, seen during summer, and Rusty Blackbird, most likely to be noted in wet areas during September-November. Western Meadowlarks formerly nested in the upper grasslands. Sadly, human disturbance resulted in nesting failures. With no young as replacements, when the last adult died, they were extirpated.

Any number of other bird species which migrate through the Calgary area are always possibilities, especially since the park has so many different habitats that could meet their temporary needs. That potential makes every visit to the area an exciting one. A bird checklist is found in Appendix II.

REPTILES Reptiles are represented by only two known species: the Wandering Garter Snake and Common Garter Snake.

AMPHIBIANS Amphibians, present on Earth for over 250 million years, have suffered sharp declines worldwide in recent years. In the park, four species of amphibians have been recorded: one salamander and three frogs. Tiger Salamander were occasional in the small pond south of the railroad tracks (South Sora Pond). Hopefully, some may still exist. Boreal Chorus Frogs, whose voice resembles a thumb running over the teeth of a comb, once common in the ponds are still found, although less frequently. The once very numerous Leopard Frog totally disappeared in the l970s almost throughout Alberta. One bright note is that Wood Frogs still occur. Their tadpoles were observed in South Sora Pond in 2001.

ABOVE *Frogs in amplexus (mating)* © Wayne Lynch
BELOW *Northern Pike* © Wayne Lynch

FISH Because of their aquatic habitat, most naturalists do not know this group of vertebrate animals very well. Fishing, mostly on a catch and release basis, is a popular activity along the Bow River. Some of the 28 species which are known to inhabit the Bow River are Longnose and White Sucker, Northern Pike, Mountain Whitefish, Spoonhead Sculpin, several species of minnows and the introduced Rainbow and Brown Trout.

INVERTEBRATES Apart from butterflies, treated in a separate chapter, no attempt has been made to catalogue the various kinds of invertebrate life occurring in the area, as far as is known. Such a list would include thousands of species.

While much is known about the animal life within the park, it is also apparent that there are large gaps in our knowledge. Anyone with time to devote to the study of any group of organisms located here can make worthwhile contributions. These would be welcomed and hopefully would be incorporated in an expanded future version of this book or published in other journals such as the publications produced by the Calgary Field Naturalists' Society.

BUTTERFLIES OF EDWORTHY PARK

By Ted Pike

Butterflies revel in sunshine. If you want to become familiar with the butterflies of Edworthy Park and vicinity, you must begin on sunny days. Consequently, if you need an excuse to get out of the house, the study of butterflies is a fine one. Besides, what better time to enjoy the area's other assets?

Butterflies tend to be active between 10:00 AM and about 7:00 PM. Most are strong fliers and rarely sit still for long. This means that you need patience if you are not going to use aids to give you a closer look. A pair of binoculars will help. You can watch butterflies while birding! Most butterfly enthusiasts carry a net and various boxes, jars or bottles, as well. There are good reasons to catch butterflies, but removing them from the park is discouraged. The net allows you to get a close look at each butterfly, and the jars or bottles will keep the butterfly safe while you identify it. Removing the lid from the jar is all you need to do to release specimens back into their natural habitat. Within a minute or two they are back about their normal business of feeding, mating, or laying eggs.

Butterflies can be seen in the park all year round but sightings between November and April are rare. Your best chances to get to know the area's butterflies are between May and August. Each month of the year you can expect to see different species, so try to get out regularly. To help get started, you may want to sign up for one of the butterfly counts held in the Calgary area. The synopsis below should help to simplify your identifications by limiting the ranges of species you expect to see. The order of presentation follows that of *Alberta Butterflies*, by Bird *et al.* [1]

SKIPPERS

GARITA SKIPPER *(Oarisma garita)*

Watch for the Garita Skipper in natural, open, grassy areas. Adults are very small, rapid fliers. They perch with their wings half open on tall flowers and grass stems. Late June and early July are the best times to see them. They are easiest to spot in late afternoon when their flight is slower.

LONG DASH SKIPPER *(Polites mystic)*

This species is named for the long black bar on the upperside of the forewing of adult males. The underside of the wings is uniformly light orange, with a bit of black at the base of the forewing. Adults frequent openings in forest cover, and edges of Aspen copses. Late June and early July are the best times to find them.

LEFT *Fritillary on Asters* © Michael Buckley

PECK'S SKIPPER *(Polites peckius)*

Peck's Skipper flies in the same habitat as the Long Dash Skipper, but will frequent mowed grass too. Males are often seen perched on lawns in cities, sunning with their wings in the typical half-open position that skippers seem to prefer.

TAWNY-EDGED SKIPPER *(Polites themistocles)*

While walking in open areas along streams or along the Bow River, you may catch a glimpse of the Tawny-edged Skipper. Adults are quite dark brown with small patches of orange on the upperside of the front wings. This butterfly tends to be rarer than its other relatives in the genus *Polites*. Careful observation should be rewarded with a few sightings of this elusive species in July.

ARCTIC SKIPPER *(Carterocephalus palaemon)*

One of our "forest" butterflies, the Arctic Skipper is best seen in shrubby openings in Aspen and Balsam Poplar forests. Adults love perching on tall leaves and flowers, but are easily startled. June is the best month to see this species in Calgary, but specimens are not common. The best area to find this species might be along Coulee Road.

DREAMY DUSKYWING *(Erynnis icelus)*

One of the first butterflies on the wing in our forested areas, the Dreamy Duskywing can be seen flitting around forest glades and border areas. Adults are easily confused with the next species, the Persius Duskywing, so catching and comparison with a good butterfly book is almost essential. Look for this species to be on the wing in May.

PERSIUS DUSKYWING *(Erynnis persius)*

Watch for the Persius Duskywing in forest clearings, and along edges of Aspen copses. You may also see adults around patches of Buffalo Bean (Golden Bean) which is the preferred larval food plant in our area. Small spots of white on the upper side of the forewing help distinguish this species from the Dreamy Duskywing. Adults are most easily seen in June.

CHECKERED SKIPPER *(Pyrgus communis)*

This is one of our grassland species, so watch for it on the fescue grassland on top of the hills on the west side of the park. Adults are fond of perching on the open ground, and can be most easily seen nectaring at flowers of Alfalfa, Aster and Fleabane. There are two broods, so if you miss this species in May and June, you can see it again in August and September.

NORTHERN CLOUDYWING *(Thorybes pylades)*

The biggest skipper in the park, the Northern Cloudywing can be found in the same habitat as the Arctic Skipper. Watch forest glades and margins for a large fast-flying dark brown butterfly. The best time to see the Northern Cloudywing is June.

SWALLOWTAILS (PAPILIONIDAE)

ANISE SWALLOWTAIL *(Papilio zelicaon)*

This butterfly is a rare sight in Edworthy Park, but it may be more common than appearances indicate. Adults are strong fliers, so a single patch of larval food plant (usually Cow Parsnip) can supply butterflies for many square miles. Watch for adults at the tops of hills in June and early July. Females may be seen frequenting sunny patches of Cow Parsnip as they seek oviposition sites. There is a rare dark form, called *nitra*, that diligent butterfly enthusiasts may be fortunate to see.

CANADIAN TIGER SWALLOWTAIL
(Papilio canadensis)

If you see a large yellow and black butterfly flying high in Aspen groves, it is almost certainly the Canadian Tiger Swallowtail. Larvae feed on Willow and Aspen Poplar. The Canadian Tiger Swallowtail is one of our most frequently noticed butterflies, for obvious reasons. Because of this, they are sometimes called Monarchs by the uninitiated. Monarchs, however, are rather rare in Alberta, and are black and orange rather than black and yellow.

ABOVE *Ted Pike (left) with Daniel befriending a Silvery Blue butterfly* © Sonia Gonsalves

WHITES AND SULFURS *(Pieridae)*

Cabbage Butterflies *(Pieris rapae)* appear in early spring, and may be seen all year long. Introduced from Europe, they have become a serious pest of market gardens, and must have been very successful during the days of the Lawrey Gardens. You can recognize the Cabbage by the presence of one or two black spots on the upperside of each wing.

WESTERN WHITE *(Pontia occidentalis)*

If you see a white butterfly following the edges of high bluffs in early spring, when Moss Phlox is flowering, it is most likely a Western White. Veins on the underside of the hind wing are outlined in dark green in early spring individuals, and light green in mid-summer and fall specimens. Eggs are laid on wild mustards.

CHRISTINA SULPHUR *(Colias christina)*

This scarce butterfly might be seen nectaring at flowers near fescue grasslands in late June and July. Males tend to be orange with black bars on the upperside. Females can also be orange, but they come in a whitish form too. Larvae feed on *Hedysarum* and *Astragalus*. Adults are powerful fliers, and rarely sit still for long.

CLOUDED SULPHUR *(Colias philodice)*

If you see a yellow butterfly on the wing in April, early May, or after August, it will be the Clouded Sulphur. Adults are avid nectarers, and will puddle in wet areas where salt seeps from the soil. Larvae are commonly encountered on Alfalfa.

BLUES, COPPERS AND ELFINS *(family Lycaenidae)*

PURPLISH COPPER *(Lycaena helloides)*

A small orange-brown butterfly, the Purplish Copper can be found in sunny areas around marshes and along riversides. They are best seen nectaring on yellow composites and thistles. Males perch on tall grass and sedge blades as they watch for females flying past. There are two broods; one in early spring, and another in August.

CORAL HAIRSTREAK (Harkenclenus titus)

This is a difficult butterfly to spot. Adults fly very rapidly, and, between flights, perch on leaves of chokecherry and Saskatoon bushes along the tops of coulees. Sometimes you can catch sight of them nectaring on goldenrod flowers near their preferred perching hosts. Watch for adults in early August.

SPRING AZURE (Celastrina ladon)

Down along the river bank, and on trails close to Dogwood, keep an eye open for Spring Azures in early May. The small blue butterflies are weak fliers, and are often seen flitting about in the underbrush before the leaves are properly out on willow and dogwood bushes.

WESTERN TAILED BLUE (Everes amyntula)

Adults in good shape are easy to recognize because they are the only blues we have that have a small, fine tail on the hind wing. Adults frequent glades and edges of Aspen forest in June and early July, where they can be seen perching on sunny leaves, rubbing their hindwings together in a manner only seen in blues.

SILVERY BLUE (Glaucopsyche lygdamus)

Silvery Blues have at least two generations each summer, so they can be seen anytime from April to August. Adults nectar on available flowers, and perch on the ground in sunny areas. The males will also puddle in wet areas where there is a bit of salt.

MELISSA BLUE (Lycaeides melissa)

The obvious orange band on the underside of the wings easily distinguishes the Melissa Blue from other Blues in Edworthy. Watch for adults nectaring on flowers near plants of the genus Astragalus in June and August.

GREENISH BLUE (Plebejus saepiolus)

Wherever there is clover, the Greenish Blue will also be found. Adults are easily seen in July and August nectaring on clover flowers. They tend to fly close to the ground, and seldom stay in one place for long.

BRUSH-FOOTED BUTTERFLIES (family Nymphalidae)

MILBERT'S TORTOISE SHELL (Aglais milberti)

Although not an abundant butterfly in Calgary, the Milbert's Tortoise Shell is easy to find near patches of Stinging Nettles that are exposed to the sun. Caterpillars are easy to find on the leaves of Nettles. Just look for leaves that are rolled into tubes. The caterpillars are inside. Adults overwinter, so they appear early in the spring and in late August.

MOURNING CLOAK (Nymphalis antiopa)

People often see Mourning Cloaks resting on gravel pathways or nectaring at thistles in August. Adults overwinter, and are among the first butterflies seen on the wing in spring. Caterpillars are communal, and can be found on willow in July.

COMPTON'S TORTOISE SHELL (Nymphalis vau-album)

Edworthy Park is one of the few places in Calgary where this elusive butterfly can be found. Best seen in early spring and in August nectaring on willows and birches that are leaking sap, you can lure this butterfly to your yard by painting a sugar solution on trees exposed to the sun.

GREEN COMMA *(Polygonia faunus)*

Eggs are laid on Bebb's Willow in the spring. Adults emerge in August and September and hibernate in brush piles, rotting logs, and other deadfall. As with all anglewings, adults are easily drawn to rotting fruit, sugar solution painted on sunny tree trunks, and Maples, Birches, and Willows that are bleeding sap.

GRAY COMMA *(Polygonia progne)*

We are on the very edge of the Gray Comma's range, so it is quite a treat to see one in the park. Adults frequent mixed forests and lay their eggs on Gooseberry. You will see them at bait stations with the other anglewings, and with Tortoise Shells and Mourning Cloaks in the spring or in the fall.

SATYR ANGLEWING *(Polygonia satyrus)*

Like the preceding species, anglewings overwinter as adults and appear in spring and fall. All anglewings will nectar at dandelions in the spring and thistles in the fall. They also puddle regularly and will come to bait in the form of rotting fruit and fresh bear and wolf droppings. Watch for them in mixed coniferous forests.

RED ADMIRAL *(Vanessa atalanta)*

Fabulous butterflies to see, Red Admirals always excite their viewers. They are not abundant, but may be seen in the spring as they come out of hibernation, and in the fall as new adults emerge. They show the same behaviours as our anglewings.

PAINTED LADY *(Vanessa cardui)*

Perhaps the most often seen butterfly in Alberta, the Painted Lady is often raised in Calgary classrooms. Some years they are quite scarce, while in other years they are everywhere in thousands. They are easily seen flying across the road and consequently, on the grills of cars. You will get the best chance to view them as they nectar at thistles, the larval food plant.

APHRODITE FRITILLARY *(Speyeria aphrodite)*

Watch for the Aphrodite Fritillary in late July or August at patches of thistles. Adults can be very difficult to distinguish from those of the Northwest Fritillary, so make sure you have one of the books about Alberta butterflies to help you. The Aphrodite Fritillary tends to be larger and females have a bright reddish brown ground colour on the underside of the fore wing.

NORTHWESTERN FRITILLARY
(Speyeria electa)

Adults of this species tend to fly a bit earlier than the Aphrodite Fritillary. Watch for them in late June and early July, although worn species hang on until the first heavy frost. All our greater Fritillaries feed on native violets as caterpillars, and you can sometimes see females walking around on the ground looking for violet plants on which to lay eggs.

ABOVE *Great Spangled Fritillary – the easiest to identify*
© L. McConnell

CALLIPPE FRITILLARY *(Speyeria callippe)*

This species and the Mormon Fritillary are the first Fritillaries on wing in the early summer. The underside of the Callippe Fritillary is one of the most silvery of all our Fritillaries, so it can be easy to recognize. Adults like high places, so you often will see them flying around the tops of hills.

GREAT SPANGLED FRITILLARY *(Speyeria cybele)*

This is our largest and darkest Fritillary. Adults love to cruise the edges of Aspen forests, and sail in and out of clearings and openings. The upperside has a dark brown colour that is missing in all our other Fritillaries. Often, in the morning, you will see them sitting in sunny areas warming up for the day's activities.

MORMON FRITILLARY *(Speyeria mormonia)*

The best way to separate the Great Fritillaries is to get one of the recent books on butterflies of Alberta or Canada. Catch a bunch of adults, sit down with the book, and work them out. Some are easily separated, but others are not. All behave about the same way and about the same time. Watch for these large brown and black butterflies with silvery spots on the underside in June and July. They love flowers, and are rapid fliers, so a net will be essential until you have some experience with them.

NORTHERN PEARL CRESCENT *(Phyciodes cocyta)*

This is our smallest brown and black butterfly. Watch for it in open grassy areas, nectaring on fleabane and yellow composites. Until this year, we thought the flight ranged from May to September. Now we know there are really two species involved, although we don't yet know how to classify them. You will see adults of one species in May, June and July and adults of the other species in August and September.

WHITE ADMIRAL *(Limenitis arthemis)*

Watch for White Admirals flying around Aspen Poplar copses and puddling in sunny wet areas. Adults are easy to spot in late June and July.

SATYRS, WOOD NYMPHS, MEADOW BROWNS AND RINGLETS
(family Satyridae)

DARK WOOD NYMPH *(Cercyonis oetus)*

Both our Wood Nymphs have a bouncy flight pattern which makes them easy to spot and identify. Dark brown butterflies bouncing over the grassy areas of the park in July and August are either the Dark Wood Nymph or the Common Wood Nymph. Dark Wood Nymphs are smaller, with a darker chocolate appearance.

COMMON WOOD NYMPH *(Cercyonis pegala)*

Large, tan brown butterflies seen in July and August are Common Wood Nymphs. Unlike the fritillaries, they don't have black spots or bars. Instead, they have one or two false eyes on the fore wing. Thistle flowers are good places to watch wood nymphs.

INORNATE RINGLET *(Ceononympha inornata)*

Adults of this butterfly are really orange. They may also have a small false eye on the underside of the fore wing. June and July are the best times to see this butterfly bouncing across the natural grassy areas of the park.

ABOVE *Wood Nymph on Goldenrod* © *L. McConnell*

RED-DISKED ALPINE *(Erebia discoidalis)*

One of our first emergent butterflies in May, the Red-disked Alpine is most commonly seen in low, wet, grassy or sedgy areas. It has the typical bouncy flight of satyrs, and it appears black when on the wing, making it easy to spot.

COMMON ALPINE *(Erebia epipsodea)*

This species is one of the most abundant butterflies in June in Calgary, and can be found easily on native grass on the west side of Edworthy Park. Adults will nectar, although it is not their favourite activity. Rather, watch for them perching on tall grass and flowers as they search for mates.

ALBERTA ARCTIC *(Oeneis alberta)*

Another one of our early spring butterflies, adults of the Alberta Arctic can be found in May on native fescue grasslands. They rarely nectar, and are most often seen sitting in short grasses along the edges of bluffs.

UHLER'S ARCTIC *(Oeneis uhleri)*

Where the Alberta Arctic is in May, Uhler's Arctic is in June. Adults will nectar and are best seen in late afternoon, when their flight is slower and they perch longer.

Footnotes – Butterflies

[1]   Bird, C.D., Hilchie, G.J., Kondla, N.G., Pike, E.M. and Sperling, F.A.H. 1995. *Alberta Butterflies*. The Provincial Museum of Alberta, Edmonton. 349 pages.

ARCHAEOLOGY AND NATIVE CULTURE

By Kate Peach and Monica Webster

REGIONAL OVERVIEW

The earliest well documented evidence for human presence in Alberta dates from about 10,500 years before present (B.P.). Evidence for occupation prior to this time is inconclusive, and may have been obscured during the glacial age. J. Chlachula believes that people made and left crude stone tools in northwest Calgary during the midst of the last glaciation,[1] but his conclusions have been contested.[2]

During the period from 10,500 years B.P. up to the period of culture contact with Euro-Canadians in the early 1800s, there is archaeological evidence of human occupation. Archaeologists generally divide the precontact past of Alberta into three distinct periods, each of which is defined on the basis of changing technological adaptations to the natural environment of the plains. These periods are the Early (11,500 to 7,500 years B.P.), Middle (7,500 to 1,750 years B.P.) and Late (1,750 to 225 years B.P.) Periods. The Late Period is followed by a short Protohistoric Period, during which historic trade goods were introduced and the Historic Period, when large scale Euro-Canadian settlement changed the nature of indigenous life on the plains.

The Early Period is first represented in Alberta by large fluted lanceolate points made and used by people of the Clovis culture. These large points would have been hafted onto a spear. It is debated whether these spears were used to stab prey or were launched through the air with the aid of a throwing stick, or atlatl. These large points were probably used by groups who occupied the fringes of lakes along the southern edge of the retreating ice sheets. As the lakes drained after the glacial period, the former lake beds became available to pioneering plant communities which supported species such as mammoth, horse and giant bison.[3] These animals provided the basis for human subsistence on the northern plains.[4] Although few Clovis sites have been excavated in Alberta, early projectile points have been found on the surface in a number of locations throughout the province.[5] Not much is known of these people's political/economic organization, resource use, or ritual life.

Following the Clovis period on the northern plains, between 10,500 and 9,500 years B.P., hunting became more specialized along the forest edge and in parkland areas, and specialized bison hunting groups emerged.[6]

LEFT *Tsuu T'ina tipis west of Calgary, 1886. Photo by Alex Ross* © Glenbow Archives NA 1494-45

By the onset of the Middle Period (7,500 BP), bison hunting was well established as the primary subsistence strategy.[7] Smaller side-notched projectile points appeared during the Middle Period. These are known as "dart" points, and were used to tip lighter spears. These spears would also have been thrown with the aid of an atlatl, or throwing stick. A number of technological changes are evident in the archaeological record. Most notable among these is the first appearance of stone circles (tipi rings) and medicine wheels, as well as evidence for communal bison hunting.

At the beginning of the Late Period a shift in technology occurred with gradual abandonment of the "dart" points and atlatl and increased use of smaller side-notched or triangular projectile points associated with bow and arrow technology. These changes coincided with the increased use of communal bison hunting strategies, such as the use of jumps and surrounds, as well as

the first evidence for the use of pottery on the plains. The technological changes are interpreted as a cultural development that developed from earlier cultural phases, combined with the admixture of bow and arrow technology from the interior of British Columbia and ceramic technology from eastern Saskatchewan and Manitoba.[8]

Table 1 outlines the major stages of Calgary's past. Phases/subphases are defined locally and are identified by the artifacts and technology seen in the archaeological record.

During the short Protohistoric Period on the plains, people continued to use Late Period technologies, with the addition of innovations resulting from indirect contact with European culture. The most notable additions to the indigenous culture were the horse, metal and other European trade goods. Evidence used to interpret this period comes from eyewitness accounts by

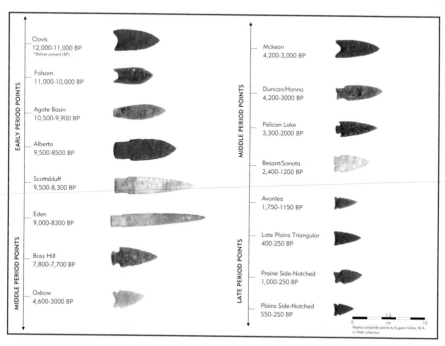

FIGURE 1 *Story in Stone Compiled by Allison Bailey*

Period	Years Before Present	Phase/Subphase
Early Precontact	10,500 – 10,000	Clovis
	10,000 – 9,500	Agate Basin and Hell Gap
	9,500 – 8,500	Cody
	9,500 – 7,750	Tuscany
Middle Precontact	7,750 – 4,000	Hawkwood
	4,000 – 3,000	Jumpingpound
	3,000 – 1,800	Paskapoo Slopes
	2,000 – 1,250	Valley Rim
Late Precontact	1,800 – 1,200	Balzac
	1,200 – 200	Old Women's

TABLE 1 *Calgary Precontact Sequence (after Reeves et al. 2000)*[9]

fur traders, travellers and historians, as well as from the archaeological record.

The Historic Period in Alberta is marked by the arrival of the first force of North West Mounted Police in southern Alberta, and the establishment of a permanent headquarters at Fort Macleod. Although European explorers and whiskey traders had entered the province prior to this period, A.D. 1874 marked the opening of the west to large scale Euro-Canadian settlement. As a result, the traditional ways of life that had existed on the plains were dramatically changed through improved transportation and communication, the near extinction of the bison, and the establishment of Treaties six, seven and nine and the consequent Indian Reservation system.

Traditionally, the Calgary region was the wintering area for the Pikani (Peigan), one group of the Blackfoot Confederacy. The Confederacy also includes the Kainaa (Blood) and the Siksika (Blackfoot). The sheltered river valley was home, as well, to a number of visiting groups including the Cree, the Atsina (Gros Ventre), the Nakota (Stoney), and the K'tunaxa (Kutenai). Tsuu

T'ina oral history recounts the splitting off of their group from northern relatives and their movement south, adopting a plains lifestyle in and around the Elbow River valley beginning in the early 18th century.

Treaty Seven was signed in 1877 by the Pikani, Siksika, Kainaa, Tsuu T'ina and Nakota. The Nakota and Pikani received the lands they requested, the Nakota in the foothills of the Rocky Mountains, and the Pikani near Fort Macleod, at Brocket. The Siksika, Tsuu T'ina and Kainaa were all placed together on one common Blackfoot reserve, which did not satisfy the Kainaa and the Tsuu T'ina. These groups preferred to stay in their traditional wintering grounds. They received those lands a few years later.

EDWORTHY PARK AND VICINITY

The area known today as Edworthy Park was called Shaganappi. This is a Cree word and means "rawhide". Bruce Starlight, a Tsuu T'ina elder, recalls his grandmother Mary One Spot stating that the word Shaganappi referred to a rawhide rope found at or near the river where there was a natural ford or river crossing. The natives may have used rope to cross the deeper parts of the swift and dangerous Bow River. The upper plateau of Edworthy Park made a perfect campground. A few archaeological sites within the park have been interpreted as campsites. The sites contain remnants of fire pits and butchered animal bone, and sometimes stone circles. Throughout the park, especially in this area, you can still see tipi rings – all that remains of tipis that sheltered families from the wind and cold.

The tipi ring stones were placed on bison hides to hold them in place. Painted designs, handed down ceremonially within families, decorated the outside. Given to the natives by the Dream Beings, the designs protected the families and each part of the design had a special significance.[10]

The natives were thankful to their Creator for the bison which supplied them with food, shelter, clothing, tools and toys. Although there are now young Aspen trees encroaching on the prairie, many of these trees were not present, even at the start of the 20th century. Prairie fires periodically swept across the land, rejuvenating the prairie grasses and preventing trees from becoming established. Fire was used as a management tool by the natives; the tender green shoots of new grass growing after a fire would attract bison. Fire may also have been used more directly to influence the movement of bison. With the scarcity of prairie fires in more recent time, aspen thickets have expanded in the area.

The Shaganappi escarpment and the Paskapoo Slopes are parts of the same escarpment and together form a bison jump (commonly known as a "buffalo jump"), similar in magnitude to other large kill sites such as Head-Smashed-In (a World Heritage Site) and Old Woman's Buffalo Jumps. The Shaganappi portion of the escarpment (between Shaganappi Point Golf Course and Sarcee Trail) was well documented as a bison jump in the early 1880s by Charles Aeneas Shaw, a CPR land surveyor who wrote:

"...a perpendicular bluff some three hundred feet high, between the foot of which and the river there was only a narrow margin. The Indians for generations had used this cliff as a pound, driving buffalo over it, killing hundreds of them at a time...; there was a large pile of bones the full length of the cliff."[11]

Although no comprehensive archaeological study has been undertaken on and below the Shaganappi escarpment, inventory reports filed with Alberta Community Development indicate the presence of butchered and burned bones, possible kill sites and boiling pits. This evidence is consistent with Shaw's description.

Documentation of the jump on the East Paskapoo Slopes portion of the escarpment (from the then-boundary of Canada Olympic Park to Sarcee Trail) was provided in an Historical Resources Impact Assessment submitted to Alberta Community Development in 1998.[12] Some 49 sites were described, including several of regional significance; apparently the slope was a massive bison jump. There is no single jump with bone piles metres deep, as at Head-Smashed-In; the jumps of Paskapoo Slopes are spread out laterally to take advantage of the many prime driving and processing areas.[13]

The Blackfoot had nine high hills used for strategic purposes. Sentinels were placed on the top of such hills and used smoke signals to warn of approaching enemies. Some sources speculate that the top of the Edworthy escarpment, known then as Shaganappi, may have been one of these "hills". Even if not one of the "nine hills", Shaganappi was undoubtedly of importance; then, as now, there is a strategic view down the river valley and north to Nose Hill.

Native peoples revered life, both plant and animal. As they traversed the prairie, they would worship the land, the plants, the bison and other animals as gifts from, and expressions of, the Spirit.

ABOVE *Balsam Poplars on Lawrey Gardens* © *Paul Beaulieu*

Footnotes – Archaeology and Native Culture

[1] Chlachula, J., 1996. "Geology and Quaternary environments of the first preglacial Paleolithic sites found in Alberta, Canada". *Quaternary Science Reviews* 16:285-313.

[2] R.R. Young, R.B. Rains and G. Osborn. 1999. "Comment on 'Geology and Quaternary environments of the first preglacial Paleolithic sites found in Alberta, Canada'". *Quaternary Science Reviews* 17: 449-453.

And

G. Osborn, L. Jackson, R. Barendregt, R. Enkin, R. Young and P. Wilson. "Geologic constraints on archeological interpretations of a Late Wisconsinan site at Varsity Estates, Calgary, Alberta". *Quaternary International* 68-71: 209-215.

[3] C.S. Churcher and M. Wilson. 1979. "Quaternary mammals from the Peace River District, Alberta." *Journal of Palaeontology*, Vol. 53, no. 1: 71-76.

And

D.A. St. Onge, 1972. "Sequence of Glacial Lakes in North-Central Alberta". *Geological Survey of Canada Bulletin* 213, Ottawa.

[4] B. Reeves, 1978. "Men, Mountains and Mammals: A View from the Canadian Subalpine". Paper presented at the Plains Conference, Denver, Co. November 1978.

[5] J.R. Vickers, 1986. "Alberta Plains Prehistory: a review." *Archaeological Survey of Alberta, Occasional Papers* No. 27. Edmonton.

[6] B. Reeves, *Op. Cit.*, 1978.

[7] J.R. Vickers, *Op. Cit.*

[8] B. Reeves, 1983. "Culture Change in the Northern Plains: 1000 B.C. – A.D. 1000". Archaeological Survey of Alberta, Occasional Paper No. 20. Edmonton.

And

G. Adams, 1977. "The Estuary Bison Pound Site in Southwestern Saskatchewan". National Museum of Man, Mercury Series. Archaeological Survey of Canada Paper 68, Ottawa

And

B. Reeves, *Op. Cit.*, 1978.

[9] B. Reeves, C. Bourges, C. Olson and A. Dow, 2000. *City of Calgary Native Archaeological Site Inventory – Draft Report.*

[10] See Niitoy-yiss: The Blackfoot Tipi Web Exhibit for a more detailed explanation of tipi designs. Glenbow Archives website.

[11] Charles Aeneas Shaw, "Tales of a Pioneer Surveyor" as quoted in City of Calgary, Parks/Recreation Department, Natural History Services, "Resources Package for Edworthy Park Area", p. 13.

[12] B. Reeves, 1998. *Historical Resources Inventory and Assessment East Paskapoo Slopes* (Permit 98 – 038).

[13] *Ibid.*

Other Sources:

W.J. Byrne, 1973. "The Archaeology and Prehistory of Southern Alberta as Reflected by Ceramics". National Museum of Man Mercury Series, Archaeological Survey of Canada. Paper 14. Ottawa.

M.W. Shortt and B.O.K. Reeves, 2001. "City of Calgary Edworthy Park Erosion Prevention Project". *Historic Resources Impact Assessment: Final Report.* Permit Number 2001-076.

HISTORY

Excerpted from Early Days in Edworthy Park and the Neighboring Areas of Brickburn and Lawrey Gardens, with additions by members of the Edworthy Park Heritage Society[1]

JOHN LAWREY AND LAWREY GARDENS

The first European settler in the area was John Lawrey[2], who arrived in 1882. He was born in 1843 in Cornwall, England. Unlike many of the early settlers of Calgary, he did not arrive from the south but from the west, having left British Columbia's Cariboo region after the gold rush. He arrived on horseback at a point just east of what is now 37th Street S.W., then close to the boundary of the Cochrane Ranche. Here Lawrey settled on the fertile river bottom sheltered by the cliff at Shaganappi,[3] an area that for centuries had been used as a native campsite and buffalo jump.

Although Lawrey arrived before the Canadian Pacific Railway, ultimately he had to acquire the escarpment lands and what would become Lawrey Gardens from the C.P.R., which had been granted the Patent to the land by the Dominion Government on December 22, 1883. Finally, in 1902, title was issued in Lawrey's name.

By the time the railway arrived in 1883, Lawrey had a flourishing market garden on the river flats. Although many people thought Calgary had a climate unsuitable for crop production, this notion was dispelled by Lawrey's efforts. John Glenn and Sam Livingston had pioneered farming to the south, but Lawrey was the first to farm the Bow Valley immediately west of Calgary. Today the river flats that bulge into the river northeast of the CPR line are still known as Lawrey Gardens.

Lawrey had a picturesque windmill, marked with his name on its vanes. Presumably, this windmill was used to pump water up over the riverbank (approximately 3 m high) and onto his land for irrigation purposes. What Lawrey apparently did not consider was that his land was on the Bow River floodplain. In a letter of December 11, 1899 to the Secretary of the Interior, Lawrey complained about the flooding of his land:

Please inform me if the Eau Claire and Bow River Lumber Company here in Calgary, can dam the river so as to cause the water and ice to flow back onto my Ranch and drown me out – half of my place today is under water – I have three root cellars full of vegetables there is a foot of water in them now the water still rising.[sic] I can't go out in to my place without going through three feet of water and ice. This is the third year this ocurred[sic] this year the worst. I have been on the place sixteen years, never had any trouble before.[4]

ABOVE *John Lawrey's house* © Glenbow Archives NA-2732-2

The Eau Claire and Bow River Lumber Company owned an island immediately to the east of Lawrey Gardens but it is unclear whether the Company's activities were the cause of Lawrey's flooding problems.

Initially, Lawrey built a log cabin on Lawrey Gardens, near the river. Later, he built a white frame house. To go into town he used an old dirt trail parallel to the railway tracks. After Lawrey spent a night out drinking, he was led home by his old grey mare – much to the consternation of friends who worried about Lawrey's safety. As recently as the 1960s, this dirt road survived in approximately the same location as the regional pathway as it enters Lawrey Gardens from the east.

When Lawrey died in 1904, his niece and nephew came to Canada and for a time, operated a gardening enterprise.[5] A succession of people – both legal owners and squatters – lived on Lawrey Gardens. Flooding was a continual problem. In a conversation with Ron Linden, Mary Dover, well-known Calgary alderman, remembered the area well. She said that when she first was an alderman, Lawrey Gardens flooded and the inhabitants were rescued. She said that there was no place for them to stay so they were put up in City Hall and there were "dozens and dozens" of them.

Eric Henson, who worked on the Rosscarrock Ranch when it was operated as a dairy by the Hilton brothers, recalled meeting one gentleman in the Holy Cross Hospital who had frozen most of his fingers before he was rescued from the roof of his house in Lawrey Gardens during one such flood. Graham Smith, the first President of Wildwood Community Association, recalls helping in the operations when the fire boats were sent to rescue people stranded by the floods on Lawrey Gardens.

So often was Lawrey Gardens flooded that finally the Province of Alberta acquired the land in 1953 and designated it as flood plain.

Of all the land in the immediate area once owned by Lawrey, today only the garden area bears his name. The rest of the property, once encompassing all the land between 37th Street S.W. and the Shaganappi Point Golf Course, and between Bow Trail and the river, is now the residential community of Spruce Cliff.

As a result of rapid urban growth and a desire to plan such growth, the City in 1911 hired Thomas H. Mawson, a world-renowned town planner. His vision of Calgary was based on the design of European cities. As part of his proposal, Mawson included the Shaganappi escarpment, Archers' Island (east of Lawrey Gardens) and Lawrey Gardens as natural areas. He described Lawrey Gardens as being exceptionally beautiful, a description which is as true today as it was then. Unfortunately, World War I intervened and the Mawson Plan was never fully implemented. Nevertheless, his vision that the Shaganappi escarpment and Lawrey Gardens should be preserved as natural areas has been largely realized.[6]

Most of the Shaganappi area to the west of what is now 37th Street S.W. was part of the Cochrane Ranche. This 109,000-acre (44,110 hectare) ranch was started in 1881 by Senator Matthew Henry Cochrane. The first two years were plagued by frigid winters and many of the cattle starved. By the summer of 1883, the ranch and remaining herd were moved to southern Alberta.[7]

THOMAS AND MARY EDWORTHY

In 1883, Thomas Edworthy, at the tender age of 16, arrived from Devonshire, England. He met John Lawrey, observed the latter's profitable market garden, and decided to follow his example about a mile to the west. Edworthy became a squatter on Cochrane Ranche land leased from the federal government and named his spread the Shaganappi Ranch.

Edworthy started with a log cabin made from Douglas-fir trees, and in 1896 built a more elaborate and still-used ranch house on the same site. The kitchen of the existing house is the original log cabin; the logs may be seen from the basement. The following year Tom married Mary Ross.

Born Mary McArthur in 1856 in Pictou, Nova Scotia, she first married Alex Ross, Calgary's first resident photographer. Part of the legacy of Alex Ross consists of the many superb photos of the Shaganappi Ranch area that still exist. Mary herself became an accomplished photographer and worked with Ross in their photo studio. In 1894, Alex Ross died of complications arising from diabetes.[8] In later years, after her marriage to Tom Edworthy, Mary acquired title to the homestead, which was in the northwest, and later sold it to the Hawkwood family.

Except for approximately ten acres, the poorer soil on the western plateau to the south of the escarpment was not tilled or ploughed. Tom Edworthy used it instead to graze his cattle. This explains why even today there is an abundance of native grass and wildflowers.

By contrast, some of the land on the river flat was cultivated. The relatively rich alluvial soil along the river was one of the secrets of success of the market gardens tended by Tom Edworthy and John Lawrey. Edworthy grew potatoes as well as other vegetables and competed with John Lawrey at the fall

TOP *Tom and Mary Edworthy with their first born son Thomas Percival* © Glenbow Archives NA – 1494 – 31

BOTTOM *Alex Ross* © Glenbow Archives NA-1494-65

agricultural fairs to see who could grow the biggest and best produce. Sometimes Lawrey won, sometimes Edworthy.

In addition to ranching and market gardening, Tom and Mary Edworthy operated four sandstone quarries through their company, Bow Bank Quarries. Shaganappi Ranch and the Edworthy family prospered. The Edworthy cattle brand was the "Lazy TE" and the cattle were grazed from the ranch on the Bow all the way south to the Elbow. The market garden vegetables helped feed early settlers and the Shaganappi Spud, which became well known, fed Colonel Steele's Scouts, residents of Fort Calgary, and other early settlers of the area.

It took some time for Tom Edworthy to acquire title to the land because he was a squatter on part of the Cochrane Ranche. He and Mary had two sons, Thomas Percival and George (Senior).

Mary and Tom Edworthy were married for only seven years when tragedy struck. In 1904, Tom Edworthy contracted typhoid fever while nursing George Livingston, son of Sam Livingston, who also had been sick with typhoid. Unlike the Livingstons who recovered, Tom died.

Without the incredible perseverance of Mary Edworthy, the ranch would not have stayed in the family. After Tom's death, the sandstone quarries were rented. Their sons helped support the family by working at various jobs while attending school. Ultimately, the family moved into town and the farmhouse and gardens were rented.

CRANDELL AND TREGILLUS: THE BRICK-MAKING YEARS

No history of the Edworthy area would be complete without reference to Brickburn, about a mile to the west of the Shaganappi Ranch house.

Originally, the area was owned by John Goodwin Watson, a man of diverse interests. Watson was born in 1858, came west in 1890, and arrived in Calgary shortly thereafter. He was a stonemason by trade. It was west of the Shaganappi Ranch house that Watson operated a sandstone quarry and also a small brick factory ("Burnvale") from 1893.[9] Watson is often called "Gravity" Watson, a nickname he earned from his efforts to construct a gravity water system that supplied the young City with its water. He was of Scottish origin and

"employed several Scots masons at the quarry and on warm summer evenings they would often break into song, to the accompaniment of bagpipes."[10] Mrs. Watson would feed all the workmen and visiting natives. Watson was elected as an Alderman in 1906. Sandstone from his quarry was used to build Central Collegiate Institute High School and, according to some sources, old City Hall.[11]

Edward Henry Crandell bought the Burnvale brick plant and surrounding land in 1905. By 1906, Crandell had incorporated the Calgary Pressed Brick and Sandstone Company "with a capital stock of $100,000 to take over 'Gravity' Watson's site".[12] This was a substantial amount of capital for the time.

E.H. Crandell was of United Empire Loyalist stock and was born in Prince Edward County, Ontario. Crandell had been mayor of Brampton, Ontario for several years before he arrived in Calgary. Here he

ABOVE *E.H. Crandell* © Glenbow Archives NA-4151-1

TOP *Brickburn* © Glenbow Archives NA-5392-5

BOTTOM *Opening of Red Cross Orphanage at Crandell House* © Glenbow Archives NA-2903-17

operated a large realty and insurance business and, like Gravity Watson, was an Alderman for a number of years. He "was a former president of the Calgary Conservative Association and contested a seat for the provincial legislature".[13]

Prior to Crandell's operation, the C.P.R. flagstation in the area had been called "Shaganappi" but Crandell was instrumental, in 1907, in having the name changed to "Brickburn". Even today there is a sign on the north side of the C.P.R. tracks marking the area as "Brickburn".

At its height, Crandell's company made 80,000 bricks per day from 15 kilns.[14] Manson states that "The 15 kilns could burn 1.5 million bricks at once".[15] Up to 100 men were employed during the summer months. There were homes for employees with families, boarding houses for single men, a post office, cookhouse, general stores, and a church.[16] Although most of these buildings were on the south side of the tracks, the post office and a small railway building were on the north side. The post office had its own postal mark, "Brickburn".

Former Calgary buildings that bore Brickburn brick included the Lancaster Building, the old Canada Customs building on 11th Avenue and 1st St. S.E., and the Capitol Theatre.[17] Still surviving examples of such buildings include the Mewata Armoury, the "Stanley House"[18] at the corner of Cameron Avenue and 10th Street S.W., and, of course, the house where Edward Crandell lived. Built by William Hextall, brother of John Hextall, the founder of Bowness,[19] the Crandell home was a three-storey, twin-gabled brick house located on the flank of Broadcast Hill. Just to the north of Edward's home was a smaller brick house (which no longer exists) where his brother Harry, the plant manager, lived. Every day, the two Crandell brothers walked down the hill from their houses to the plant.

In 1920, the Crandell house was leased by the Red Cross for use as an orphanage. Opened on July 14, 1920 by R.B. Bennett,

"Brickburn House" or "Soldiers' Childrens' Home", as it was known, provided accommodation for 60 children.[20] There was a school on the premises. Two and a half years later Brickburn House was closed. From 1931 to 1935, Crandell's sons lived in the house.[21] Ultimately, it was sold to Judge Henry Stuart Patterson (after whom the community of Patterson Heights is named) and then to Stu and Helen Hart. The house is well known today as home of the Hart family who have lived there for about 50 years.

The bricks made at Brickburn were stamped "E.H.C." for Edward Henry Crandell or "Calgary" for "Calgary Pressed Brick and Sandstone Company". Generally, they were a reddish orange color, although some of the bricks were a darker brown. You may see this contrast if you look at Mewata Armoury and at the Crandell house itself. In addition to the red brick made at Brickburn, the plant also produced a high quality, green, enamelled, decorative brick. The only examples of this known to us are in the facings of two fireplaces in the Crandell house. The Brickburn plant was "one of four institutions of the kind on the continent capable of turning out the high class enamelled brick and encaustic tile…".[22]

Crandell was also involved in exploration for oil and the drilling of the first oil well in Alberta in the Waterton National Park area. As a result of his business activities there, a mountain, a lake and a nature interpretive centre are named for him in Waterton National Park. In addition, one of the buildings at SAIT in Calgary is named after him. Crandell died in 1944 at the age of 85.[23]

About a mile to the west of Brickburn was another brickmaking enterprise. Although Brickburn was in operation from 1905 to 1931, the Tregillus Clay Products plant only operated for two years, from 1912 to 1914. W.J. Tregillus, from Devonshire, arrived in Canada in 1902, and bought some of the flatland above Spruce Cliff. His property included what is now part of Rosscarrock and Westgate, and that part

of Wildwood south of Spruce Drive. He operated the Rosscarrock Ranch and imported purebred Holstein cattle for breeding and milk production. According to Jack Peach, Tregillus was the first dairy man in Calgary to pasteurize milk and deliver it in bottles.[24]

The Rosscarrock Ranch house was an elegant two-storey red brick house. It was north of the present Bow Trail and between 37th and 38th Streets S.W. but unfortunately was torn down in the 1960s.

Tregillus was well known for his efforts in dairy farming and for establishing the elevator system for grain storage. With a group of leading farm representatives, he spearheaded discussions about "the possibility of shipping Alberta grain west to the nearest tidewater rather than the traditional route east to the head of the Great Lakes".[25] He was the president of the United Farmers of Alberta from 1912-1914, and the first president of the Farmers' Co-operative Elevator Co., which, after a merger in 1917, became the United Grain Growers. In addition, he was a City alderman, an executive of the Calgary Horticultural Society, and the president of a choral society.[26]

The brick plant was a victim of the outbreak of World War I and, soon thereafter, Tregillus's death. Despite his tremendous generosity and his substantial assets, Tregillus died virtually bankrupt because his other assets had been frozen with the onset of World War I. The Arts Building at the University of Alberta, the Holy Trinity Church in Edmonton,[27] and a few buildings in Calgary were built with brick from his factory.

It is ironic that some of the Tregillus bricks were used to build the first academic building at the University of Alberta because

TOP LEFT *W.J. Tregillus* © Glenbow Archives NA 2784-4

TOP RIGHT *Tregillus Clay Products* © Glenbow Archives NA 3050-15

BOTTOM *Rosscarrock Ranch* © Glenbow Archives NA-4066-1

one of the causes championed by both Tregillus and Crandell was the establishment of a university in Calgary. Both Crandell and Tregillus donated substantial sums of cash as well as land: Crandell's land on what is now Broadcast Hill and Tregillus's land on the Rosscarrock Ranch. Early subdivision plans for the Broadcast Hill area – optimistically called Varsity Heights – show proposed streets that were named "Varsity" and "College", for example. In 1910, a "charter for the college was obtained from the Sifton government and classes were held in the basement of the Public Library".[28] The institution ran for three years but ended with the onset of World War I.[29] Calgary would wait for an autonomous university until the early 1960s.

FROM RANCH TO PARK

In 1963, George Edworthy Sr. sold Shaganappi Ranch to the City of Calgary. The City Council resolution authorizing this purchase refers simply to buying the land "for civic purposes".[30] Graham Smith states that it was thanks in large measure to Harry Hays, then mayor of Calgary, that the City purchased this area. Harry Hays had piled a number of Aldermen into his car and had taken them to the area and said "Now lads, we have a good opportunity to buy this land".[31] It was revolutionary for the City to buy natural areas because until this time, the notion of "park" had been restricted to groomed parks and facilities to keep kids off the street.[32] At that time, Graham Smith was a political reporter for the *Albertan* and has written that Hays "suggested in a private conversation to me …that the area could make a good open space".[33]

A letter from the City Clerk to Harry Boothman, Parks' Superintendent, dated October 1, 1962 stated that at "the Special Council meeting held on September 29th, the following motion was adopted: 'That the Shaganappi Ranch, recently acquired for civic purposes, be named Edworthy Park'".[34]

Although no specific use was mentioned in the Council resolution authorizing the purchase, the area was soon claimed by Engineering as a potential site of an expressway, Shaganappi Trail, and just as quickly claimed by Parks and Recreation as a natural area park. Photos of early signs from the 1960s label the area as Edworthy Park. Harry Boothman, Director of Parks and Recreation, was responsible for having signs installed which read: "Edworthy Park – Yours to Use & Enjoy Now To Protect & Preserve For the Future". Other uses proposed for the area over the years included a sewage treatment plant.[35]

In 1972, construction began on the first Douglas Fir Trail using student labour under several programs and grants. The western entrance to the trail begins just to the east of what is technically Edworthy Park. The Douglas-fir escarpment legally was not part of Edworthy Park. When the communities of Wildwood and Spruce Cliff were created, it was reserved as "Environmental Reserve", that is, as undevelopable land due to steepness, stability and hydrology concerns. Small portions of the slope were part of the Community or Municipal Reserves of Wildwood and Spruce Cliff.

In 1994, the Douglas Fir Trail, which had fallen into disrepair, was rebuilt by the City of Calgary, with participation by the Edworthy Park Heritage Society and more than 1,000 volunteer hours. It was financed in part by generous donations from the Community Facility Enhancement Program, Brawn Foundation, an anonymous donor, and Alberta Sport, Recreation, Parks and Wildlife Foundation. Edworthy Park (the area immediately to the east of Sarcee Trail), the Douglas Fir Trail and Lawrey Gardens were designated in the 1990s as a Major Natural Environmental Park that now is used by thousands of people annually.

From its rich native history to its more recent ranching, quarrying, and brickmaking history, Edworthy Park and its neighbouring areas of Paskapoo Slopes, Brickburn, Lawrey Gardens and Shaganappi Slopes have a wealth of history to be explored.

ABOVE *The original Douglas Fir Trail, circa 1970s* © Bill Robinson

Footnotes – History

[1] The Society is indebted to Ron Linden and Jill Clayton who wrote the sections on Lawrey Gardens and Brickburn respectively in *Early Days in Edworthy Park and the Neighboring Areas of Brickburn and Lawrey Gardens*. The section on Edworthy Park and the Shaganappi Ranch was compiled largely from George Edworthy Sr.'s diary at the Glenbow Archives. We are also indebted to George Edworthy Jr. for clarifying certain points. The present overview has been expanded by Society members to include additional information about W.J. Tregillus and E.H. Crandell.

[2] His name was misspelled in various City documents as Lowery but his birth certificate gives the spelling as "Lawrey".

[3] Shaganappi was the area which extended from what is today Shaganappi Point Golf Course at the east along the escarpment west to the area now bordered by Sarcee Trail S.W.

[4] Letter from John Lawrey to Secretary, Department of the Interior, Dec. 11, 1899. It is believed that the original of this letter was on file in the Provincial Archives, Edmonton and was subsequently quoted in a Royal Commission on the Flooding of the Bow River in the early 1950s.

[5] Based on research by Ron Linden.

[6] City of Calgary Archives, Thomas H. Mawson & Sons, *The City of Calgary: Past, Present and Future* (City of Planning Commission of Calgary (Alta.), (1912), in Town Planning Commission, Box 1, File 6, p. 48.

[7] Glenbow Archives History, Cochrane Ranche fonts, p.1.

[8] There is also a collection of photographs taken by Alex Ross at the Provincial Museum, Winnipeg, Manitoba. Some of Ross's photos were acquired by Harry Pollard and are at the Provincial Museum in Edmonton.

[9] Jack Manson, *Bricks in Alberta*, p. 91.

[10] Marie Riley, "City Woman Recalls Grandparents' History," *Calgary Herald*, Jan. 9, 1967. [1/9/67]

[11] City of Calgary Archives Website, *John Goodwin Watson*, Aldermanic Gallery, Also mentioned in Marie Riley, *Op. Cit.*

[12] Jack Manson, *Op. Cit.*, p. 89.

[13] Obituary, "Founder of Brickburn Dies. E.H. Crandell" *Calgary Herald*, May 6th, 1944.

[14] *The Morning Albertan*, "The 100,000 Manufacturing, Building and Wholesale Book Edition, 1914.

[15] Jack Manson, *Op. Cit.*, p. 89.

[16] *Ibid.*

[17] Jack Peach, "Crandell Homes Characterized by Solid Workmanship", *Calgary Herald*, Sat. July 11, 1981.

[18] *Ibid.* Jack Peach elaborates that the Stanley House was built for David S. McCutcheon from Brickburn bricks by Mr. T.E.A. Stanley a teacher and later principal of Western Canada High School.

[19] Jennifer Bobrovitz, "Crandell House", *Calgary Herald*, Sun. Feb. 14th, 1999.

[20] *Ibid.*

[21] *Ibid.*

[22] *The Morning Albertan*, "The 100,000 Manufacturing, Building and Wholesale Book Edition, 1914.

[23] Obituary, "Founder of Brickburn Dies. E.H. Crandell", *Calgary Herald*, May 6th, 1944. [5/6/44]

[24] City of Calgary Archives, Reference File, W.J. Tregillus, article by Jack Peach, "If the job needed doing, W.J. Tregillus was there", *Calgary Herald*, undated.

[25] *Ibid.*

[26] *Ibid.*

[27] It is believed that this is the Lutheran "Trinity Church" in Edmonton (the first brick building of this church having been constructed in 1914) and not the Anglican church "Holy Trinity" as the bricks for the latter were carried up in wheelbarrows or carts by parishioners from a brick plant in the Edmonton river valley.

One of the buildings in Calgary built from Tregillus's bricks is the Lorraine Apartment Building (unattributed manuscript on W.J. Tregillus, Glenbow Museum Archives)

[28] Georgina Thomson, "Colorful Rosscarrock", *Calgary Herald*, 31st May 1958.

[29] *Ibid.* Grant McEwan also recounts the history of Calgary College in his book, *Calgary Cavalcade*, pp. 130-131.

[30] City of Calgary Archives, Meeting of Calgary City Council, 1962.

[31] Graham Smith, in an article written to the Society, 2002.

[32] *Ibid.*

[33] *Ibid.*

[34] City of Calgary Archives, Letter from City Clerk to Mr. Harry Boothman,October 1st, 1962, in City Clerk's Correspondence, 1962, Box 27, File 7.

[35] Graham Smith, *Op. Cit.*

ABOVE Police Car Moth on Goldenrod © Paul Beaulieu

LEFT Looking east down the Bow River with Douglas-fir trees on Wildwood escarpment in background © Paul Beaulieu

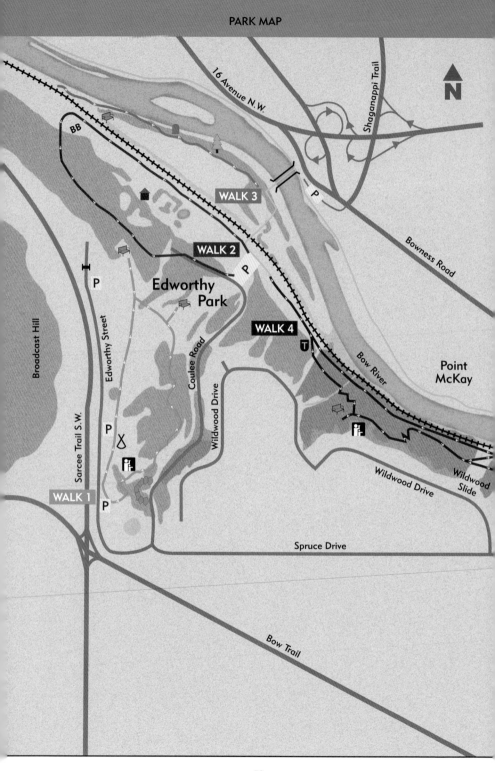

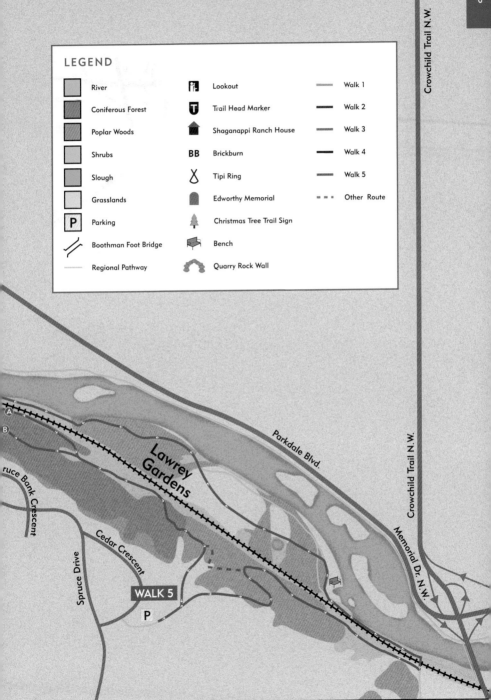

LEGEND

River	Lookout	Walk 1
Coniferous Forest	Trail Head Marker	Walk 2
Poplar Woods	Shaganappi Ranch House	Walk 3
Shrubs	BB Brickburn	Walk 4
Slough	Tipi Ring	Walk 5
Grasslands	Edworthy Memorial	Other Route
P Parking	Christmas Tree Trail Sign	
Boothman Foot Bridge	Bench	
Regional Pathway	Quarry Rock Wall	

Crowchild Trail N.W.

Parkdale Blvd.

Crowchild Trail N.W.

Memorial Dr. N.W.

Lawrey Gardens

Spruce Bank Crescent

Cedar Crescent

Spruce Drive

WALK 5

P

THE WESTERN
PLATEAU

WALK ONE

OVERVIEW

A gentle but long walk leads across the upper plateau of Edworthy Park through a native prairie fescue meadow and aspen woodland. The route goes eastward to the Coulee's edge then north to the major north-facing escarpment, and finally loops back to the south. On this walk, we explore the geology and the archaeology of the area. Fragile grasses and a multitude of wildflowers can be observed. The traditional uses of local flowering plants, and associated native legends, passed down as oral history, are recounted.

BELOW *Prairie Crocus* © Paul Beaulieu

STARTING POINT:

At the western end of Spruce Drive S.W., turn left (west) onto Edworthy Street and follow it around the bend to the first parking lot. Two trails lead from the north end of the lot. One heads north, parallel to Edworthy Street; another heads left (northeast) into aspen trees beyond the meadow. Take this second trail.

Before you start your walk, notice the plaque-bearing boulder 8 m east of the parking lot. The smooth surface of the rock to the upper left of the plaque is marked by shallow, faint striations and deeper gouges. Although the coarse marks could have been made by a bulldozer[1], most of the fine gouges were made in glacial times as the boulder was ground against bedrock or other rocks as it moved with the ice.

On leaving the parking lot, you are surrounded by the immensity of a large prairie – a typical fescue prairie rich in a variety of native grasses and wildflowers. Racing across the prairie's broad expanse, the wind makes ripples like ocean waves in the native grasses. It sweeps across a land that was home to the Plains Indians. As you walk through the meadow of Edworthy Park, feel the wind and sun and experience the glory of a prairie.

Prairies (treeless areas) are defined by their grasses. Short grass prairie, centered around southwestern Alberta and southeastern Saskatchewan, is technically the arid phase of the mixed grass prairie. If you move outward to the east, increasing precipitation creates the tall grass prairie of Manitoba. As you move west, towards the mountains, increasing precipitation creates the fescue prairie of the eastern slopes. In Calgary, where prairie meets foothills, the prairie is neither shortgrass nor tall grass but is in between.[2] Here, the dominant

species of grasses are the fescues – hence the name, fescue meadow. Rough fescue, the most common fescue species in the Calgary area, grows here with its distinctive bunches and bluish hue. The edges of a blade of this grass feel rough.[3]

There are additional species of grass here. You may remember Spear Grass from your childhood – it is present, as are Blue Grama Grass, June Grass, Northern Wheat Grass and several others. These grasses are adapted to dryland conditions. One adaptation is their long roots enabling them to reach moisture deep below the surface. In bunch grass systems, the key winter survival mechanisms are the growing points, which are right down near the ground in the well-insulated crowns, and the phenomenally well adapted physiology and metabolism of these grasses.[4]

One of the glories of the prairie is the great diversity of plant life. Unlike a domesticated lawn, which is a monoculture with one species, the fescue meadow has many different species within a small area.

As spring arrives, the brown grass of the previous year dominates the landscape. The first green plants appear in April. The Edworthy plateau is known for its Prairie Crocuses. As you leave the parking lot, in early spring, you see the purple sweep of crocuses in bloom. The name 'crocus' is a misnomer because these plants are really anemones. Unlike the cultivated crocus, Prairie Crocus does not grow from a bulb but from seed. If each park user were to pick one flower, thus eliminating the plant's chance to set seed, future park visitors would be deprived of seeing this harbinger of spring.

As crocuses emerge, their downy stems appear. This "down" consists of many small hairs which cover the plant. The hairiness serves two purposes – first, to trap the sun's heat, and secondly, to catch dewdrops so that the plant has water in the arid early spring.

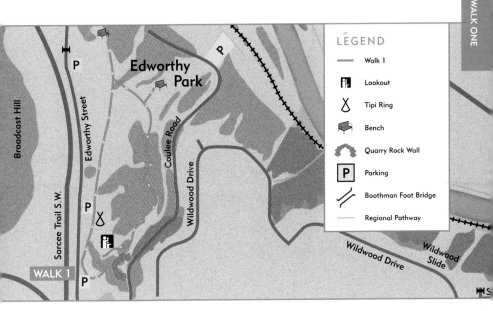

LEGEND

▬	Walk 1
🗒	Lookout
⋀	Tipi Ring
🪑	Bench
⋒	Quarry Rock Wall
P	Parking
⫻	Boothman Foot Bridge
──	Regional Pathway

Another adaptation is in the structure of the seed with its long twisted hairs. These hairs act as a wick for moisture after the seed has fallen to the ground. When there is sufficient moisture, they untwist like a corkscrew, driving the seed into the soil to enhance the likelihood of germination.

There is an alternative explanation for the crocus's hairiness. Native history describes how Wapee went on a vision quest. No visions occurred to him in his search for contact with the Great Creator. In his isolation in the mountains, he befriended a small white flower who told him many things and gave him the visions he sought. Wapee protected his friend from the cold with his robe. The Great Creator was pleased with Wapee's kindness. Wapee asked the Creator to grant the little flower three wishes. The flower wished that it might have the colour purple of the mountains, a sun for its heart and a warm coat like Wapee's robe. As recounted by well known Alberta artist and author, Annora Brown, in her classic book, *Old Man's Garden*, this is the story of how the crocus obtained its colour and its warm coat.[5]

Elsewhere in the park, the crocus grows not only in prairie fescue-grassland areas, but also on north-facing slopes interspersed with juniper and Kinnikinnick (Common Bearberry).

Continue from the parking lot until you reach the edge of the aspen forest and descend into a shallow gully. This gully is a tributary or branch of the main coulee (hereafter referred to as "the Coulee") that descends to lower Edworthy Park. Keep to the right pathway as you ascend the small rise.

To your left, as you leave the woods, in mid-summer you will see a shrub-like plant called Spreading Dogbane. Its name indicates a plant that dogs should avoid. The flowers are like delicate pink bells. Plains Indians used the milky sap to "clean buckskin"; also, in moderation, as a hair tonic.[6] The "bark" of the stem provided cordage and is used by birds such as orioles to weave their nests.

As you proceed along the path, on your right, across the gully, you see some exposed rockfaces of Porcupine Hills Formation sandstone. These are the

THOS. EDWORTHY.

Bow Bank

Sandstone Quarries......

SAMPLES

May be seen in P. Burns' Residence
and in the Norman Block

TOP *Spreading Dogbane* © L. McConnell
BOTTOM *Bow Bank Quarry business card* - Glenbow Archives, Edworthy file

remains of Edworthy's main quarry – the most visible of the four quarries operated by Thomas Edworthy and his company Bow Bank Quarry. This quarry supplied the sandstone that completed the Alberta Legislature Building when the Glenbow quarry near Cochrane went out of business before construction was finished. Several other buildings were constructed from Bow Bank sandstone – notably, the CPR station in Vancouver, the Lougheed, Clarence and Norman Blocks in downtown Calgary, the residence of Senator Pat Burns and several schools and churches.[7]

Even today, you may see the marks in the sandstone where the quarry workers used long metal rods to pry the sandstone boulders out of the quarry. Once the

sandstone was pried from the rock face, it was cut into smaller blocks. For this, stonecutters used saws with metal blades. These saws were continually wetted to prevent the blades from overheating from friction. It was gruelling work.

After this was done, the sandstone was transported to market. George Edworthy Jr., grandson of Thomas Edworthy, described how there were three derricks designed to lift the sandstone and load it. Two of these derricks were on the west side of the road, just beyond the west rim of the Coulee, while a third derrick was on the east side of the road up the coulee wall. The derricks were connected by cable. Buckets suspended from the cables were filled with sandstone and slid along the cables to be unloaded. The sandstone was then transported by rail to its destination. After Thomas Edworthy died in 1904, the quarry was rented first to William Oliver and then to Gilbert, Bone and Leblanc.[8] This provided some income to Mary Edworthy who had two sons to support.

Proceed along the rim trail for a short distance. As you approach the rim of the Coulee, small cliffs just below the trail on the right reveal the local geology in cross-section. The plateau traversed by this route is a large bedrock bench on the east side of Broadcast Hill, intermediate in elevation between the Bow River floodplain and the top of the Hill. The bench likely was cut by an ancestral version of the Bow River as it was incising into the old Broadcast Hill/Nose Hill surface. Bedrock, however, is not found right at the plateau surface because the rock is covered by two layers of surficial sediment, visible in these cliffs. The lowermost of these two is a densely packed gravel layer about one metre thick, resting on the sandstone. This gravel has all the earmarks of river gravel (particularly the roundness of most of the stones) and may have been deposited by the same river that cut the bedrock bench.

Most of the stones in the gravel are of a rock

type called quartzite, which is formed as sandstone is buried and metamorphosed. Many or most of the quartzite cobbles we see here, and elsewhere in Calgary, are derived from a geologic unit called the Gog Group, a package of metamorphosed sedimentary rocks that crops out in the Rockies along and near the continental divide. This means that the stones we now see in Edworthy Park must have traveled a long distance down the Bow River drainage, via rivers and/or glaciers, possibly from the Lake Louise area. The sand grains that now constitute the Gog Group (and the cobbles below the trail) were deposited in a shallow sea in Cambrian time, roughly half a billion years ago.

Here, and elsewhere on the upper plateau, you may notice that many pebbles and cobbles are partly coated with a white crust. The crust is calcium carbonate, or limestone, which precipitates out of groundwater in semi-arid climates like that of Calgary.

The uppermost of the two surficial units overlying the sandstone here is a layer of fine-grained sediment one to two metres thick. It is mostly silt, a grain size intermediate between sand and clay. This sediment is most likely wind-deposited silt, known to geologists as "loess". Such silt deposits are common just below the ground surface in many parts of Calgary. They indicate that the several thousand years following the ice age were a very dusty time.

A typical prairie soil is developed in the loess and can be seen in the small cliffs below the trail. It consists of an upper, dark gray "A" horizon, overlying a reddish-brown "B" horizon, overlying a horizon containing flecks of white – the same calcium carbonate that coats many of the pebbles.

Near the quarry viewpoint, on a late June walk, you will see beautiful blue lupines which predominantly grow in this portion of the park. There are several lupine species in Alberta. This one is the Perennial or Silvery Lupine.

What is intriguing about a lupine is that its six to nine fingered-leaves follow the sun. "The leaves especially are continually on the move, the many fingers opening and closing, or moving horizontally with every passing change of light and going quite obviously to sleep at the approach of nightfall".[9] Also intriguing is the plant's ability to hold a jewel-like drop of water in these finger-like leaves.

In this same area, in summer the lovely blue flowers of the Common Harebell will enchant you. The very fine upper stems, according to author Annora Brown, reminded early Scots of hair. Annora Brown also noted that their spelling of "Harebell" left something to be desired since it should have been "Hairbell".[10] The origin of the common name remains a mystery. Although Brown offers one explanation, R.G.H. Cormack in his classic book, *Wild Flowers of Alberta*, suggests that the word "harebell" is a "contraction of heatherbell".[11] The *Oxford Dictionary of English Etymology* suggests that "hare" is a very old Latin word for "hoary".[12]

ABOVE *Silvery Blue Lupines* © O.F. Wachtler

TOP *Common Harebell* © E. Gilliam

MIDDLE *Edworthy Coulee and Coulee Road* © J. Osborn

BOTTOM *Fossil leaf in sandstone, Edworthy Park* © Sonia Gonsalves

Look for harebells throughout this area, especially at the southern portion of the park.

Approach the rim of the main Coulee, and look down into the largest of the valleys cutting back into the Bow River escarpment. The word "coulee" is French for "couler" meaning "to flow" and refers to the water that flows down a coulee valley. [13]

Because the mouth of the Coulee (at the parking lot at the bottom of Coulee Road) is at the level of the modern Bow River floodplain, the Coulee was probably cut in post-glacial time, during or after the Bow cut down through glacial deposits to its current level. The Coulee is presently the main transportation route between the upper and lower levels of Edworthy Park, and Wilson[14] surmises that it was also a transportation route in prehistoric times, for both native peoples and bison. Certainly, in more modern times, it is documented that there was an old Indian trail in the Coulee.

Here, looking down, you can see prominent outcroppings of sandstone of the Porcupine Hills Formation. Here, as elsewhere throughout the park, fossilized plants have been found embedded in the sandstone.

Beyond the eastern rim of this Coulee, and to the south, there was a "buffalo rubbing stone" which was dynamited during the construction of the community of Wildwood. Bison would come from kilometres away to rub against the stone. Obviously, on the "bald" prairie, stones large enough for a bison to rub against were rare and bison would travel to such stones, wearing trails into the land. "Before so much of our native grasslands disappeared under the plough, these trails could be seen radiating in all directions across the prairie."[15]

Continue northward along the path that follows the Coulee rim. There are a variety of possible trails in some places, but basically stick to the rim. The cliffs overlooking Coulee Road show that a few metres of gravel overlie the sandstone in this area. On the opposite side of the Coulee, below a white-painted fence, the slope above the road has been stabilized by the City of Calgary using geo-textiles.

Slightly to the south (right) of the white fence on the other side of the Coulee, hidden by the trees, George Edworthy Sr. and his family had a summer house for many years. The house was built of materials from hangars from Calgary's original airstrip in what is now Westgate district. Little remains of this house, which burnt down in the 1940s.[16]

As you continue north along the path, where it forks, take the lower (right) path just below the rim. In early June, you will see a small patch of blue flowers of the genus Penstemon, Smooth Blue Beard-tongue. This is one of the loveliest prairie plants. Although previously there had been about 20 plants in this location, in 2001 we could

ABOVE *Edworthy summer house – the "cabin".* © George Edworthy Jr.

find only six of them on the east-facing sunny grassland slope. Sadly, uncontrolled erosion of the pathway (due to shortcutting) will lead to their total loss, unless active control measures are put in place.

Although several penstemon species grow in the mountains and the foothills, this species is a hallmark of the prairies. Although now spelled "penstemon", it originally was "pentstemon" which referred to "five stamens". According to Annora Brown, the fifth stamen is usually sterile and bearded, thus the alternate name of Beard-tongue. Penstemon species range in colour from "white to yellow, rose, purple and darkest ultramarine".[17] The species found in Edworthy is *Penstemon nitidus*, with greyish-green, lance-shaped leaves.[18] Penstemon is a favourite flower of hummingbirds.

As we walked here in mid-June 2001, the penstemons were just going out of bloom. At the same time, we saw Common Blue-eyed Grass plants in bloom nearby. The small, blue star-shaped flower which sits on a slender blade of grass is difficult to miss. It is not a true grass but a member of the Iris family.[19]

Near the penstemons, on the edge of the lower trail, rests a two-metre-long quartzite boulder covered with at least two different species of lichens. How did this boulder get here? It is almost certainly a glacial erratic, transported from the mountains within or on the surface of glacier ice.

This boulder is part of a narrow string of such boulders derived from the Gog Group

LEFT *Smooth Penstemons* © Gillean Daffern
RIGHT *Blue-eyed Grass* © O.F. Wachtler
ABOVE *Wild Licorice* © E. Gilliam

of quartzites, described earlier. The string, formally named the "Foothills Erratics Train", extends from the Edson/Hinton area down to northern Montana. The largest member of this train is the Big Rock near Okotoks. The prevailing theory of origin is that landslide debris in Jasper National Park was carried eastward by a glacier filling the Athabasca River valley. That mountain ice was forced southward by the Laurentide Ice Sheet emanating from central Canada, whereupon the quartzite boulders were strung out along the interface between mountain and continental ice. The boulders came to rest as the ice ultimately melted away.

Continue north along this path. In mid-summer, the sharp eye will also spot Common Blue Lettuce. The plant possesses a milky, latex-like sap. Just beyond this plant one may also see Wild Licorice. Annora Brown describes how Native Americans roasted the root as a staple food and how it supported explorers from Mackenzie to Lewis and Clark. In July, look for its pale yellow, almost white, pea-like bloom.[20]

Keep right on the rim trail until you can see, for the first time, a bit of landscape on the north side of the Bow River. Across the Coulee can be seen scattered outcrops of Porcupine

Hills sandstone, and a few muddy spots where water seeps out of the sandstone.

In this vicinity, the path is bordered by Wolf Willow (also called Silver Berry). Wolf Willows are not willows at all but are members of the Oleaster Family. In early June, you can smell its pungent fragrance on the wind. Some describe it as overpowering or cloying; others as sweet. After blooming, the flowers are transformed into powdery, silver "berries". Inside, there is a shiny narrow, oblong brown seed striped with yellow. These seeds were used by Plains Indians to make necklaces and to decorate the fringes of their clothing.[21]

Follow the trail until it arrives at two relatively large spruce trees, among the stunted aspen, on the edge of a small coulee tributary to the main Coulee. The view beyond the two spruce trees is of the west wall of the Coulee. At the base of this wall, in 1939/40, George Edworthy Jr. found buffalo skulls exposed by floodwaters receding in the coulee. Not only was the north-facing escarpment a buffalo jump, but so also may have been the Coulee. A small path descends steeply downhill but we will stay on one of the main trails which bends left and follows the rim of the tributary coulee to arrive back at the rim of the main Coulee.

Our walk passes through a mixed aspen forest with plants very different from the prairie ones we have just seen. No longer are we in an exclusively dryland area – here, the plants reflect the presence of more moisture. In the 1960s, there were not as many aspens here as today. Prairie fires protected the grassland from encroachment by trees.

The lack of fires in recent years has allowed the slow but steady incursion of the aspens into the prairie grasslands. Ironically, however, when aspens are destroyed by fire, a hormone signal which normally "inhibits growth of additional stems" is destroyed by fire so the "result is a dramatic increase in the number of new trunks sprouting".[22]

Here in summer you may see a small bird catching insects on the wing. The Least Flycatcher is skilled in aerial manoeuvres, catching insects in mid-air. An aspen grove bordering an open field is a favourite territory of the Least Flycatcher. If you are close enough, you may see its very distinctive eye ring. In addition to catching its food on the wing, the Least Flycatcher also "searches under leaves for caterpillars, ants and other insects" and sometimes eats berries.[23] It is marvellous seeing the fly-catcher's acrobatic skills in operation!

As you pass through the grove of aspen trees, a faint breeze may cause the leaves to start "trembling". One of the names for Aspen Poplars is, indeed, Trembling or Quaking Aspen. The leaves stir in the slightest breeze because the petioles or leaf-stems are flat. Its grey catkins supply a wealth of food in the spring to a great variety of insects and birds. There is little which rivals the beauty of the first green as aspen leaves unfurl before many other plants have come to life once again.

Although an aspen tree individually has a life span of only 60 years, it is but one stem of a clone that can regenerate itself almost indefinitely. Aspen trees sucker with each tree within a clone or colony being joined to

TOP Bison skull found by George Edworthy Jr. at base of Coulee Road 1939/40 © Edworthy Park Heritage Society

BOTTOM Saskatoon leaf in autumn, © Paul Beaulieu

another. Each sucker is genetically identical to the others – that is why the aspen trees in a group turn colour at the same time and seem to be painted in the same shade of yellow. The aspen tree is responsible for saving many a native who ate the inner bark roasted during famine years.[24] It is believed that the white powder on aspen trees serves as protection for the tree from the sun and was used as a sunscreen by natives.

Ecologists have long recognized the value of mixed aspen woodland for the shelter and food it provides for many species of mammals, birds and butterflies. Enjoy the beauty of the lovely white tree trunks and the first tender green of spring in this area.

In late May and June, you may hear a Yellow Warbler singing nearby. Bordering the trail are wild roses in profusion, some Heart-leaved Alexanders and a patch of Canada Anemones. With broad but sharply indented or serrated leaves, this woodland anemone is easily distinguished from others, – for example, the prairie Cut-leaved Anemone. The large white bloom (2 to 4 cm in diameter) of the Canada Anemone provides a marked contrast to the various shades of green in the woodland forest.

Here, also, smell the perfume of wild roses on the breeze. In late June, the woods are full of this Provincial Flower of Alberta. Native peoples used them in many ways – the rose hips were used as a source of vitamins while the roots were used for cosmetic purposes.

Nearby you may see in early June, twining around a tree or shrub, the tendrils of a Purple Clematis vine. The introduced ground-hugging Yellow Clematis may be seen nearby in the fescue meadow in late summer. Here the shade and moisture encourages the Purple Clematis.

Another vine here is one that ends in a single large cup-like leaf, from the centre of which spring yellowish-orange flowers. This vine "twines" its way around trees and shrubs. As you walk along the escarpment path in June, watch for many of these Twining Honeysuckles.

After passing along and through trees for a considerable distance, the trail reaches the northern edge of the aspen forest. A right fork of the trail continues along the rim but now take the left fork, along the edge of the aspens, soon crossing a multi-track that projects to a point left of the University of Calgary campus in the distance. Shortly after crossing the multi-track, the path goes

TOP *Wild Roses* © Paul Beaulieu

MIDDLE *Wild Bergamot or Monarda* © Gillean Daffern

BOTTOM *Twining Honeysuckle* © O.F. Wachtler

downhill slightly to the west. Here in mid-summer, in the small vale to the left, you note a colourful patch of Wild Bergamot with rose-coloured flowers. The meadow is a lively palette splashed with the rose-pink of Wild Bergamot and the blue of Wild Flax and Harebells.

In June, here you may see Common Alpine butterflies. A medium-sized butterfly, the Common Alpine is very eye-catching with its chocolate brown background and colourful orange bands surrounding small eyespots.[25]

In the distance, to the west, a dense patch of thistles provides larval food and, later, nectar for the adult Painted Lady Butterfly.

Painted Ladies flying through the park! Can any phrase more colourfully describe this brilliant orange butterfly? If you read a book on butterflies, one thing will strike you, in addition to the colourful beauty of the butterflies themselves – that is the colourful and fanciful names of the butterflies. In these books, the etymology (the study of the origin of a word) is as colourful as the entomology (the study of the insects)!

Not only is the common name, Painted Lady, colourful, so also is its scientific name, *Vanessa cardui*. As is explained in the book *Alberta Butterflies*, the genus name "Vanessa" refers to a "mystic divinity of the Orphic rites in ancient Greece".[26]

Painted Lady butterflies are bright orange with distinctive markings of "dark brown on the dorsal [top] wing surface". On the ventral or lower side, this butterfly has two large "eyespots" and three smaller ones.[27] Unlike Mourning Cloaks and anglewings, this butterfly does not overwinter in Alberta but migrates here from the southern United States. Some years their population in Alberta will be sparse, other years plentiful. Seen on the upper plateau several times, on each occasion, it has been visiting the flowers in a thistle patch. Thistles, which we might think of as inhospitable, are much beloved by this butterfly in both its adult and larval stages. Its species name, *cardui*, in fact, means "wild

TOP *Painted Lady butterflies migrated en masse to Alberta in 2001* © O.F. Wachtler

BOTTOM *Insect on Northern Bedstraw* © E. Gilliam

thistle". The adults also visit flowers of alfalfa and clover as well as garden plants. Their caterpillar eats plants in the thistle, borage, mallow and pea families.[28]

Our path goes west, around the head of one of two medium-sized coulees extending from the picnic areas of lower Edworthy Park into the escarpment. Shortly before the trail enters the next grove of aspen, it intersects a multi-track running northeastward, toward a couple of benches, with the Trans-Canada Highway in the distance beyond. We will take a short detour from our main loop along this multi-track trail.

Along this trail, on a summer's day, you may not only see Painted Lady butterflies, but also Rhombic-leaved Sunflowers with their sunny yellow glory. Once on this path in July, a Milbert's Tortoise Shell butterfly landed at our feet.

Throughout these sunny areas of the upper plateau, from late June, bloom the white

TOP *Fritillary basking in the sun* © O.F. Wachtler

MIDDLE Moss Phlox © Paul Beaulieu

BOTTOM *The nodding blossoms of Three-flowered Avens*
© O.F. Wachtler

clusters of Northern Bedstraw. This sweet-smelling flower was, indeed, used as straw for the mattresses of pioneers. In addition to supplying a soft and sweet-smelling resting place, Northern Bedstraw was used by settlers as a source of red dye. It is a member of the 'Madder Family' from which the ancient dye madder was obtained.[29] The roots were used by Plains Indians to dye porcupine quills. Northern Bedstraw draws many insects to its flowers.[30]

Here also you may see a variety of orange butterflies marked with what seems like a confusing array of brown markings. With careful study, you may learn to distinguish the various species, but to simplify matters, these are Fritillaries. The name of the subfamily is Argynninae, Greek for "silvery", as the ventral (underside) of the wings is marked with "silvery reflective patches".[31] The brown markings of the Fritillary provide almost perfect camouflage when the butterfly sits with open wings on a sunflower.

The sunny meadow is perfect terrain for Atlantis, Aphrodite, Freija or Meadow Fritillaries with their lovely names. Here is Aphrodite, named after the "Greek goddess of love and beauty who sprang from the foam of the sea".[32] Flying past, is Atlantis, named after the "mythical lost continent of the Atlantic Ocean".[33] Perhaps Freija sits with its wings open as fritillaries love to do when they bask and feed at a flower – it is the namesake of a Norse goddess of love and fertility![34]

As you continue northeastward on the narrow strip of meadow between two coulees, in early spring, you might find one of the earliest of all spring flowers, Moss Phlox or *Phlox hoodii* with its tiny white flowers and ground-hugging foliage.

Again, in early spring, this hillside is blanketed with crocuses. To the left (west), in June, you may see large patches of Three-flowered Avens. With their three nodding rosy-red blooms, they seem to be asleep. As the flowers age, however, the heads stand upright pointing to the sky. There are several

ABOVE Western Wood Lily, increasingly rare © Wayne Lynch

other common names for this plant – among which are Prairie Smoke, Old Man's Whiskers, and Lies on its Belly. Certainly, the long, persistent stiles look like whiskers!

Later in the summer, until the end of July, look downhill along this same east-facing slope and you will see a wonderful patch of Yellow Umbrella-plants. With its clusters of yellow flowers forming an umbrella over a single stalk, the yellow umbrella gradually turns pinkish red as it matures. This is the only known area of the park in which umbrella-plant, a member of the wild Buckwheat Family, is found. It is a delight to see the little umbrellas marching, as it were, up the grassy slope!

In the same area, you may have the good fortune to see a pale yellow paintbrush. Common Yellow Paintbrush is more frequently found in the foothills and prairies than in the mountains where the red species seem to predominate. It takes but little imagination to envisage the brush dipped into paint! Some paintbrushes are parasitic plants, and depend on raiding the water and perhaps nutrients from nearby plants. They flourish by maintaining a careful balance – with the host plants – a balance which enables them to thrive while ensuring that their hosts survive.[35] Although not all paint-

TOP Common Yellow Paintbrush © E. Gilliam
BOTTOM Yellow Umbrella-plant © E. Gilliam

TOP *Common or Wandering Garter Snake* © Wayne Lynch

MIDDLE *Early one morning, Silvery Blue butterfly waits for the sun.* © L. McConnell

BOTTOM *Melissa Blue* © Paul Beaulieu

brush species are parasitic, several are dependent on other plants in this way.

Paintbrush is not the only plant with requirements in this regard. In the soil are mycorrhizae (fungi) essential to the survival of many prairie plants. Sometimes, individual species of mycorrhizae are necessary for specific plants. Scientists have only begun to recognize this interdependency between plant, soil and its microscopic organisms. One reason why many transplanted prairie plants do not thrive in gardens is that this complex composition of prairie soil cannot be duplicated.

At the benches at the end of this path, pause for a moment and enjoy the view. This was a strategic view for the natives, who could see for many kilometres from this vantage point. To the north, they could see the vast expanse of what is today called Nose Hill. They had a panoramic view of the river valley. The view was essential to protecting the native inhabitants from invading strangers. It was probably for strategic reasons that, along the crest of the escarpment, there are three tipi rings. Here, also, at the edge of the cliff, you can appreciate why this escarpment was part of an extensive buffalo jump.

Enjoy the panoramic view of the river valley, northwest Calgary and downtown, and then retrace your steps back to the trail intersection where this detour began. Now turn right (north-westward) into the second grove of aspens, crossing another shallow gully. This gully is the upper part of the second of the two medium-sized coulees. Well downstream in this coulee a spring marks the head of a perennial stream that flows down to the base of the escarpment. Our trail emerges from the gully onto grassland where it merges with the main multi-track that heads north from the first and second parking lots.

Continue straight ahead (northward) on the main trail. The trail passes to the left of a small glacial erratic, composed of quartzite as usual. This one is angular, about half a metre long, and encrusted with white calcium carbonate. The trail then descends slightly and reaches the main Bow River escarpment where two benches are situated.

To the left (west) in this area and along this escarpment in general, you may see – from your location on the path – the now rare Western Wood Lily (the wild "tiger lily" of our youth!). Unfortunately, the children of the 1960s and 1970s who picked the Wood Lilies did not know that picking the flower dooms the plant to death. When picking the flower, you inadvertently pick the leaves that store the food for the bulb. Without food from these leaves, the bulb dies. If you are fortunate enough to see a Western Wood Lily, please do not pick it. Save the plant for your children and theirs to enjoy.

Near the bench, we once observed a large snake crossing the path. To this day, we think that it was too large for a Garter Snake, although we did not stop long enough to make a positive identification. The sandstone outcrops of the escarpment are used by hundreds of Garter Snakes as hibernacula. The snakes hibernate in these locations to survive the winter. When spring arrives, they make a mass exodus and gain the body heat they need to mate, by basking in the sun.[36] Perhaps the snake we saw was the grandmother of all Garter Snakes...

A constructed trail descends the escarpment from this point and ultimately intersects with the Pond Lookout Trail, which is described in the next section of our trail guide. For now, however, turn back the way you came, following the main north-south multi-track trail back to the parking lot.

As you head south, in the open meadow, you may see many little blue butterflies. This section of the fescue meadow abounds with Blues. It is as if atomic fragments of the blue prairie sky are flitting through the air. One of the earliest families of butterflies to be seen in Edworthy (soon after Mourning Cloaks and anglewings), the Blues are prolific here and make a June walk delightful.

It is difficult to distinguish the many species of blue butterflies found in the area.

ABOVE *A female Swainson's Hawk sits on her nest.* © Wayne Lynch

Identified on the butterfly count undertaken for this book were several Silvery Blues. With its wings closed, this butterfly has pale silvery or grey underwings. A row of black spots encircled with white rims is near the margins of the wings. This butterfly is a denizen of meadows but also of many other habitats such as woodland clearings. [37] Look carefully and if you see the smallest of tails on the bottom edge of its wings, you are watching a Western Tailed Blue, a butterfly which likes the meadows and clovers found here.[38] You may also see a blue butterfly sitting with its wings closed – wings bordered by a row of orange spots. This is the Melissa Blue.

As you continue southward, you may see colourful patches of pinkish blue vetch. Its common name is American Vetch. These plants greatly enliven the prairie and add nitrogen to the prairie soil. Vetches are also an important food source for some butterfly families.

Overhead, you may see a Swainson's Hawk. Its nesting area is nearby and the open prairie is prime hunting territory.[39] You may also see a pair of Red-tailed Hawks, flying, circling, or hovering overhead. This also is their traditional hunting ground as they search for Richardson's Ground Squirrels and other prey. A flash of sunlight may illuminate the

TOP *Purple Prairie Clover* © E. Gilliam

MIDDLE *American Goldfinch (male)* © Wayne Lynch

BOTTOM *Brown-eyed Susan (Gaillardia)* © Urs Kallen

distinctive "brick-red upper tail".[40] The Edworthy upper plateau is an ideal habitat for the Red-tailed Hawk since this species prefers woodland near open space.[41]

As you walk, look closely and again you may see Common Blue-eyed Grass. Later, this trail is bordered by Purple Prairie Clover. Although classified as a member of the clover family[42], this plant does not suggest clover to us. Its flower suggests a coneflower but in this case the lower buds open first with a "circle of flowers moving gradually upward"[43] to form a purple cone of bloom. Its stems are covered in "down" or hairs[44], like other drought-tolerant plants. After many other flowers have gone to seed, the Purple Prairie Clover is just coming into bloom and lends its beauty to late summer.

Walking back, at the height of summer, watch for the bright yellow of a male American Goldfinch. Perched on the stem of a sow thistle, the Goldfinch may suspend itself upside down as it tries to extract seeds from a neighbouring plant. It is a great show of gymnastics!

The upper plateau of Edworthy Park is almost synonymous with summer. As summer arrives, the yellow of its hot sun in the blue sky is mirrored by the sunny yellow of Gaillardia. From afar, its orbs of yellow rays look like small suns suspended in the prairie grass. Just as the Crocus defines the springtime, so the Gaillardia defines the prairie summer.

In June, here we saw a small lovely butterfly called an Inornate Ringlet. As the name suggests, it is not ornate but has a subtle beauty with pale orange on the underside of the forewing seen when its wings are together. On the orange is a small eyespot.[45]

Later, on a hot July day, we also saw Painted Lady butterflies, a newly emerged Mourning Cloak, Fritillaries, and Wood Nymphs. These latter butterflies are brown with pale blue eyespots bordering the edge of the upper wings. There is a noticeable difference between the sexes, females being a lighter brown and larger.[46]

ABOVE *Sunbeam on Inornate Ringlet butterfly* © E. Gilliam

Along much of the return trail, the upper soil has been eroded away by human and dog traffic, exposing the quartzite cobbles that normally lie below the surface. The rounding of these cobbles and the little chip marks found on many of them suggest that river water once flowed across here. The chip marks are thought to be formed as stones collide with each other while being moved at the bottom of a river.

You may note tiny shards of bone in patches of freshly turned soil. Who is the mysterious creature that is creating these small piles of loam? This is the work of the Northern Pocket Gopher, seldom seen, as it is subterranean. In doing their excavations, pocket gophers often "unearth" bone fragments from buffalo hunts of days gone by.

Pocket gophers play an important role in the prairie grasslands by keeping "soil porous and arable by their burrowing. They turn over three to six tons of soil per acre". Here is the rich moist soil they prefer.[47]

In addition to the mounds of pocket gophers, you may see the ubiquitous holes of the Richardson Ground Squirrels – commonly but incorrectly known as gophers. Although almost everyone is familiar with ground squirrels, few people are familiar with their natural history. Primarily herbivores, ground squirrels eat "mostly plants such as roots, bulbs, stems, leaves and seeds. Less commonly, they also eat insects, birds' eggs and young birds".[48]

We are all familiar with the sight of a ground squirrel standing guard at its burrow hole. It has emerged from its burrow "after

ABOVE *Standing at attention! Richardson Ground Squirrel*
© Wayne Lynch

hibernating all winter in a coma-like state". The ground squirrel, with its high-pitched whistles, is one of the harbingers of spring.[49]

The City in recent years has poisoned ground squirrels, which is a great pity. These animals are a crucial link in the food chain of other animals – notably many species of hawks, and coyotes, weasels and badgers. The poison also kills these predators or scavengers or negatively affects their reproduction.

In the vicinity of the second parking lot, you will encounter a very large Indian tipi ring – about 11 metres in diameter. This ring may have been used for Council meetings as it is larger than the rings used for shelter by a family. George Edworthy Sr. remembered being told, when he was growing up, that council meetings were held at this ring.

Stones in the interior of the ring complicate the picture. Bruce Starlight, an Elder of the Tsuu T'ina Nation, theorizes that it may not be a Council tipi ring but rather a medicine wheel. He points out that if it were a tipi ring, there would be no stones in the interior of the circle. By contrast, interior stones would be consistent with a medicine wheel used for sacred, ceremonial purposes. Medicine wheels had spokes of stones radiating from the centre on north-south and east-west alignments.

Just to the northeast of the large stone ring, before the aspen grove, there were bison wallows. In spring, bison would wallow in the shallow depressions to rub off old fur by rolling in the dirt. The wallows may have been used by the bison to kick earth on themselves to discourage insects. Unfortunately, these wallows were filled in but their location may be determined by looking to the northeast where there is a patch of grass different from the rough fescue of the prairie. The taller domesticated grass is clearly visible.

To the east, opposite the second parking lot, you may also see a small plant with grass-like leaves and a cluster of tightly packed white flowers. This is the highly poisonous Death Camas. Earlier along this trail, you may have seen a larger plant with more loosely arranged white flowers. This is White Camas, also poisonous. Both are in the Lily Family.

These plants underscore the notion that you should never eat (and perhaps not even touch!) a plant unless you are sure that it is safe to do so. What looks vaguely like an onion may in fact be a deadly camas bulb.

We can imagine what life was like for native peoples inhabiting this plateau of prairie grasslands. Native culture was sophisticated in its use of plants for medicinal and cultural purposes. They certainly knew to avoid eating the deadly White and Death Camas plants. Yet Blue Camas with its similar looking bulb, found further south in the Province, was a prized food over which wars were fought.[50]

With their sophisticated knowledge of plants, natives knew which plants were poisonous, and which were used for food, medicine and religious ceremonies. Some parts of the same plant were poisonous while others were edible. Native knowledge obviously included practical information about how and when to harvest the plant, whether or not to dry the harvested plant in the sun, etc. Only relatively recently has the science of ethnobotany endeavoured to document the scientific basis of medicinal native plant use. There is much to learn and much that may already have been forgotten.

As you walk through the prairie grasslands, notice how sensitive the prairie grass is to trampling. Herds of bison from time immemorial have not caused the amount of sustained damage to the wildflowers that off-trail use is causing. How, you may wonder, can people, bicycles and dogs damage a park where thousands of bison once roamed?

The answer is given, in part, by Don Gayton in his book, The Wheatgrass Mechanism, when he considers "why the prairie grasses survived grazing by free-ranging bison but do so poorly when grazed in pastures by domestic cattle". He states that:

When a big herd did stop to graze, chaos would reign. Grazing pressure was incredible; new leaves, old leaves, dead stems and seed heads were all either eaten or mashed into the ground. Shrubs were broken off and trampled. Vast quantities of manure and urine were laid down and the surface soil was thoroughly stirred up. In a very few days nothing edible would remain and the herd would leave. Then, because of the massiveness of the western space, three, five, even ten years might elapse before another herd would return to that same site.[51]

This is the difference, then – a large herd of bison might only infrequently visit what we enjoy now as Edworthy Park as opposed to the continual heavy use, and unfortunately, abuse, that the park now receives.

Don Gayton discusses how fragile the prairie grasses are:

Buffalo grazed and rolled and trampled and dunged their way over this land for ten thousand years, and would have had a profound effect on our vegetation. The native grasses of buffalo range should be well adapted to these grazing animals, since we know that buffalo eat grass almost exclusively. Curiously, though, many of our native grasses seem exquisitely sensitive to grazing of any kind.

If these grass species – the fescues, stipas and wheat grasses – evolved hand in hand with the shaggy buffalo, why then are they so fragile? Why do they decline so quickly under modern cattle grazing, to be replaced by other, less desirable vegetation?[52]

As you walk along the trail, please remember that the native prairie grasses which abound in this part of Edworthy Park are sensitive and fragile. We can lose the great diversity of a prairie fescue meadow if people shortcut through it. We can lose many of the wildflowers that grow next to trails if people step on them or pick them.

RIGHT *White Camas* © O.F. Wachtler

The treasures of the fescue meadow will not endure unless preserved by a conscious attempt on the part of all users to stay on the trails. The plant trampled by an unthinking footstep, the flower snapped off by the wheel of a bicycle or a bouncing ball, the plant torn out by the rear paws of a dog racing uphill may never bloom again. On an individual basis, these seem like trivial things but the *cumulative* effect is a threat to the survival of this area in its native form and to the survival of ground-nesting birds and other wildlife found here. As recently as five years ago, the lyrical song of the ground-nesting, beautiful Western Meadowlark was routinely heard in this area. Now, the meadowlarks are gone, extirpated from Edworthy Park.

Although Rough Fescue has recently been designated as the official grass of Alberta, still Alberta is rapidly losing its fescue prairie fields and meadows to development. How fortunate we are to have a living piece of history right here. There is an urgent need to preserve this area – please join us in preserving the Edworthy fescue meadow and its wildlife now and forever.

Continue to the south. You may get back to the first parking lot by veering to the right (west) on a multi-track and passing through the Balsam Poplar trees very near Edworthy Street. The trees sit in a depression that is part of the same tributary coulee crossed very near the beginning of this loop. Large sandstone boulders resting in the bottom of the depression are by-products of the construction of Edworthy Street.

TOP *Early Cinquefoil* © M. Bailey

MIDDLE *Hoary Puccoon* © Paul Beaulieu

BOTTOM *Grass in Winter* © Paul Beaulieu

RIGHT *Awash in a sea of fleabanes, near the Yellow Umbrella-plants* © M. Bailey

Footnotes – Walk One

[1] Although typical of Porcupine Hills sandstone, this rock was not originally from Edworthy Park but was donated by a developer.

[2] Don Gayton, *The Wheatgrass Mechanism*, p. 23, and also in correspondence from Don Gayton to the Edworthy Park Heritage Society, August, 2002.

[3] Calgary Field Naturalists' Society, *Nose Hill: A Popular Guide*, p.66.

[4] Don Gayton, *The Wheatgrass Mechanism*, p. 24.

[5] Annora Brown, *Old Man's Garden*, pp. 13-15.

[6] *Ibid.* pp. 99-100.

[7] James Dempsey, "The Thomas Edworthy Quarries", June 1984, Historic Sites, Alberta Culture (now Alberta Community Development), p. 5.

[8] *Ibid.* p. 2.

[9] Annora Brown, *Old Man's Garden*, p. 160.

[10] *Ibid.* pp. 38-40.

[11] R.G.H. Cormack, *Wild Flowers of Alberta*, p. 334.

[12] C.T. Onions, editor, *Oxford Dictionary of English Etymology*, p. 427.

[13] Thomas Willock, *A Prairie Coulee*, pp.19-20.

[14] Michael C. Wilson, *Once Upon a River*, p. 412

[15] Don Gayton, *The Wheatgrass Mechanism*, p. 100.

[16] In conversation with George Edworthy Jr., June, 2002.

[17] Annora Brown, *Op. Cit.* pp. 190-193.

[18] Vance, Jowsey, McLean and Switzer, *Wildflowers Across the Prairies*, p. 250.

[19] George W. Scotter and Hälle Flygare, *Wildflowers of the Canadian Rockies*, p. 154.

[20] Annora Brown, *Old Man's Garden*, pp. 55-57.

[21] *Ibid.* pp. 228-229.

[22] Wayne Lynch, *The Great Northern Kingdom. Life in the Boreal Forest.* p. 16.

[23] Federation of Alberta Naturalists, *The Atlas of Breeding Birds of Alberta*, p. 183.

[24] Annora Brown, *Op. Cit.*, p. 249.

[25] C.D.Bird, Hilchie, Konda, Pike and Sperling, *Alberta Butterflies*, p. 294

[26] *Ibid.* p. 227

[27] *Ibid.* p. 229.

[28] *Ibid.*

[29] Annora Brown, *Op. Cit.*, p. 118.

[30] *Ibid.* p. 119.

[31] Bird, *et al.*, p. 231.

[32] *Ibid.* p. 247.

[33] *Ibid.* p. 249.

[34] *Ibid.* p. 239.

[35] C. Dana Bush, *The Compact Guide to Wildflowers of the Rockies*, p.52

[36] A.P. Russell and A.M. Bauer, *The Amphibians and Reptiles of Alberta*, pp. 176-178.

[37] Bird et al., *Alberta Butterflies*, p. 191.

[38] *Ibid.* pp. 189-190.

[39] Federation of Alberta Naturalists, *The Atlas of Breeding Birds of Alberta*, p. 86.

[40] *Ibid.* p. 87.

[41] *Ibid.*

[42] Annora Brown, *Old Man's Garden*, p. 128.

[43] *Ibid.* p. 129.

[44] *Ibid.*

[45] Bird et al., *Alberta Butterflies*, p. 288.

[46] *Ibid.* p. 287.

[47] CFNS, *Nose Hill: A Popular Guide*, pp. 106-107.

[48] *Ibid.* pp. 110.

[49] *Ibid.*

[50] Annora Brown, *Old Man's Garden*, pp. 43-46.

[51] Don Gayton, *The Wheatgrass Mechanism*, p. 104.

[52] *Ibid.* p. 102

BRICKBURN & POND
LOOKOUT TRAIL

WALK TWO

OVERVIEW

Before we begin walking, we consider the geology of the area. The route then leads past the Shaganappi Ranch House to the site of the old brick plant at Brickburn. Turning left to go part way back up the hillside, the route passes through an aspen forest and then some upland Balsam Poplars far removed from the river. Several species of wildlife call this area home. Because of the variety of habitats converging in this area, it is a great route for the hiker to see a variety of migratory birds, especially warblers and hawks.

BELOW *Porcupine eating rosehips* © Wayne Lynch

STARTING POINT:

Start from the main Edworthy Park parking lot on the south side of the railway tracks. To reach the lot, turn right at the west end of Spruce Drive S.W., and continue down Coulee Road ("Edworthy Park" on the present street sign). Alternatively, if approaching from the north side of the river, go to the southern end of Shaganappi Trail N.W. past Bowness Road to Montgomery View. Proceed by foot across the Harry Boothman Bridge to the lot south of the river.

The parking lot is situated on a fan-shaped deposit extending from the mouth of the Coulee north to the CPR tracks. The deposit is called an alluvial fan because it consists of stream sediment ("alluvium") derived from the Coulee. The volume of sediment in the fan is not enough to account for all the missing rock whose erosion created the Coulee, so it is likely that much of the Coulee erosion happened thousands of years ago, with the resultant sediment washing down the river. After much of the Coulee had been eroded, the flat bench of river sediments was deposited on what are today the picnic areas. Continued erosion in the Coulee in more recent times is responsible for the fan, which at least in part overlies the flat bench. A storm sewer trench dug across the fan in the 1970s was examined by archaeologist Michael Wilson; he found a bison skull at a depth of 3.6 m. A radiocarbon age indicating the skull dates from the first century A.D. confirms the relatively young age of the visible fan deposits. Because of its alluvial location and nature, Wilson described this area as being of considerable archaeological interest.[1]

From the parking lot, walk north (toward the river), past the chain-link fence on the north side of the lot, then turn west on an old dirt road (now parallel dirt tracks) between the fence and the railway tracks. After a few hundred metres, the fence on the left becomes partly engulfed in trees and shrubbery. Ultimately the fence ends. Just ahead on the left are two upright posts, formerly some of the gateposts of the Shaganappi Ranch House which is about 100 metres off to the southeast, at the base of the scarp. You may not be able to see it clearly from this vantage point because of the trees and shrubs. The farmhouse is a typical prairie clapboard house with twin gables. After the Edworthy era, the house was used by several other families. Although the farmhouse is now a provincially designated Historic Site, it is rented to private tenants and not open to the public – please respect their privacy.

It was on these river flatlands that Tom Edworthy grew hay for his cattle, and vegetables in his market garden. Old photos show one of the original barns in this area.

By the 1880s, bison had all but disappeared in North America – a catastrophe for native peoples who relied on the bison for food, clothing, tipis, tools and toys. The native peoples were facing starvation and imported disease. When Thomas Edworthy grew the "Shaganappi spud" in the 1880s and 1890s, he was helped with the harvesting by some of the Tsuu T'ina people. Their lifestyle had radically changed in a very short period and now they, too, depended on spuds and other agricultural produce and income from work here and in the nearby town of Calgary.

As you continue west along the dirt path, you pass through an area bordered on the left by hybrid poplar trees. To the right, the path is bordered by grasses, some native, some not. Nearby, to the left (south), in late June you may notice a fairly large plant with clusters of white blooms – this is a large specimen of Drummond Milkvetch.

On a July day, you will notice low roses blooming near the ground. These roses have white instead of the usual pink blooms. Hugging the ground, these short white roses

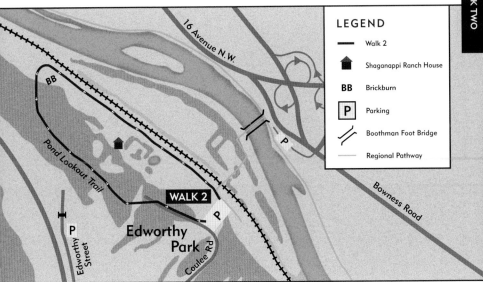

LEGEND

— Walk 2

🏠 Shaganappi Ranch House

BB Brickburn

P Parking

Boothman Foot Bridge

---- Regional Pathway

are a native Prairie Rose, *Rosa arkansas*, and add a touch of delicate beauty to the walk.

This is butterfly territory! In summer, you may see several different species. There are many little blue butterflies. Also watch for Inornate Ringlets with pale orange upper wings.

Here, too, Painted Ladies which we also encounter on the upper plateau, enjoy the grassy territory. White Admirals fly past. They are unmistakable with their black background and white band near the margin of their wings. If you are close enough, you may observe a row of beautiful blue spots under a row of rusty orange spots. Truly, this makes an admirable butterfly – indeed the name "Admiral" is a corruption of the original name, "White Admirable".[2] As this is another transition zone – so typical of the park where grassland meets woodlands – there is an abundance of butterflies.

Once while walking here on a July day, we thought we saw a Painted Lady butterfly. Upon closer inspection, we realized that it was its close relative, a Red Admiral butterfly. Red Admirals are well known for their friendliness and may land on you. Like the Painted Lady butterfly, they migrate to Alberta from the United States.[3]

Continue westward. You are soon walking where the old beehive kiln and drying shed of Brickburn once were located. The kiln was called a beehive kiln because of its shape. Many Calgarians were familiar with the area and several have recounted how during the Depression their families lived on stew made from rabbits hunted in this area.[4] After the plant stopped operating, "Mrs. May Hutton, her sister Lil and a number of other people ("the gang") used the area to ski in between 1937 and 1939". The Brickburn skiers would ski out along the railway tracks to "the

ABOVE *White Admiral butterfly* © Urs Kallen

cabin" which they rented for $6.00 a month from Harry Crandell. In summer, the Eaton's Hiking Club hiked out to the Brickburn area and used this same cabin.[5]

Proceed until just before you reach a fork in the trail, in front of an old metal gate partly hidden in the trees. The low grass- and shrub-covered rise to the left (south) of the fork may look like a natural hill but actually consists of some of the remnants of Brickburn which have been covered by soil.

Look closely. On the side of the mound, you will see bricks or shards. Some bricks are marked EHC (for "Edward Henry Crandell", the plant owner), others "Calgary" (for "Calgary Pressed Brick and Sandstone Company"). The red brick is a remnant from the Brickburn plant that was in operation from 1905 to 1931. Most of the metal machinery was sold for scrap metal in the war years but, even yet, you may see the odd metal door or other relic. Please leave all materials – including any bricks and fragments – as they are for the next person who comes along to see them.

The clay in the hillside above was considered ideal for brickmaking. Today if you stand on the north side across the river, and look back, you may easily discern where the clay was excavated on the south escarpment.

Although there was a fair-sized brick plant and operation here, the area has been revegetated with native trees, bushes and wildflowers over the years to such an extent that one really has to be alert to notice that there was such an operation in what today is a natural area.

Before leaving Brickburn, note that about a mile further to the west, also on private property, was the site of W.J. Tregillus's brick plant, the Tregillus Clay Products Company. Although only in production for two years, the Tregillus Clay Products Company produced sufficient bricks for several buildings. For a period of four years, Tregillus owned the Bowness Ranch and lived in the ranchhouse built by John Hextall at the east end of the Ranch – also about a mile from where you are standing.

At the opposite end of the greater park area, just below Shaganappi Golf Course, Tregillus had another facility. Although there is reference to this on legal titles (and various sources have mentioned it), it remains unclear whether this was a kiln or a clay extraction facility.

Tregillus's Rosscarrock Ranch and dairy continued to operate after the brick plant closed. After Tregillus's death, the Hilton brothers, Bill, Jimmy and Geordie operated a dairy farm there for several years.

On leaving Brickburn, take the left (south) fork at the old metal gate. Do not proceed further west as it is private property. The trail bends southward under the power line and begins climbing the lower part of the scarp in a southeasterly direction. This trail is known locally as the "Pond Look-Out Trail". Here one morning, a mother Mallard led the way followed by her ducklings and then by us. It is unusual – and charming – to have a duck as a trail guide!

On this section of trail, we once saw the brilliant blue of a Belted Kingfisher as it darted to the Balsam Poplar forest next to the river. Such Balsam Poplars are perfect perching sites. The riverbanks form ideal nesting sites as kingfishers dig "a burrow in a steep vertical bank, preferably one close to water and fishing areas".[6] Its magnificent blue and white plumage is unmistakable. As you climb Pond Look-Out Trail, you may indeed see kingfishers flying back to the riverbank as they often return to their burrows year after year. Certainly, the fishing is good for kingfishers nearby as there is a plentiful supply of small fish.[7]

In a tree in the vicinity of Pond Look-Out Trail, near the power pylons, there is a Swainson's Hawk nest. These world travelers migrate to Argentina, using "favourable winds in their migration". This hawk catches grasshoppers, ground squirrels, jackrabbits, mice, etc. It hunts

TOP *Swainson's Hawk chicks* © *Wayne Lynch*
BOTTOM *Short-tailed Weasel* © *Wayne Lynch*

from a perch or from the air. Swainson's Hawks are among our larger hawks.[8]

In June, the song of a thrush called Veery may be heard, especially at dusk. The hauntingly beautiful flute-like "veery, veery, veery, vaary" rolls and descends in scale with an echo-like quality. Although it may sound a long way off, it is quite close, the voice like a ventriloquist's. Other birds usually heard singing along the trail here are the Warbling Vireo and Red-eyed Vireo. As with the Veery, it takes skill to see them.

Several mammals inhabit the mixed aspen forest in this area. Although more common several years ago, weasels may still occasionally be seen here. They eat insects, ground-nesting birds, hares, ground squirrels and mice. In turn, they are preyed upon by coyotes, foxes, hawks, owls, cats and dogs.[9] It is possible to see three species in Edworthy Park – the Least Weasel rarely

exceeding 20 cm in length and, more commonly, the Short-tailed and the Long-tailed Weasels. Both inhabit open country, aspen woods and river bottom.[10] This route passes through ideal weasel country.

During the early days of Edworthy Park, and even as recently as the 1960s and 1970s, lynx were found in the park. Certainly, in years of famine due to a hare shortage in the mountains and foothills, lynx follow the river valley and on rare occasions might be seen here. Similarly, cougars, bear and moose were seen in the park in the years immediately following the development of Wildwood and other neighbouring communities and still might be seen today. In recent years, on at least one occasion, an unmistakable set of bear paw prints has been noted!

Occasionally, even yet, you may see a badger trundling through the woods at dusk. The American Badger is a feisty creature, although he plods along. Badgers are great diggers, and live in large burrows, the entrances to which are "obvious because of the great mounds of excavated earth". Among other things, they eat ground squirrels, pocket gophers, mice and ground-nesting birds.[11]

More commonly encountered than lynx, badger, moose and bear, are porcupines. Here, as elsewhere in the park, you may notice aspens or willows with the bark chewed off high up. This results from the efforts of porcupines which also have a fondness for apple trees. In winter, porcupines eat the tender inner bark – the cambium layer – of aspen trees. Each spring, the mother gives birth to a solitary offspring. The "pup" is "playful in contrast to its solemn parents".[12] This area is ideal for porcupines – they may wander into the nearby communities – as dog-owners there already know.

Other mammals that may be seen in this area include skunks. Although they have become much less common in Edworthy Park after the development of Coach Hill,

more skunks may find their way into the park due to disturbance from new developments to the West.

Where the trail levels out, views open up to the residence-covered flatlands on the north side of the river. Those flatlands constitute the Bow River floodplain. A floodplain is defined as "a plain that floods", a definition perhaps under-appreciated by floodplain developers and residents in Calgary. There were major floods in Calgary in the late 1800s and early 1900s, but none since 1932. As few Calgary residents today were here in 1932, there is a perception that either the Bow River does not flood, or that

TOP *American Badger* © Wayne Lynch
BOTTOM *A skunk explores in the woods* © Wayne Lynch
LEFT *Bohemian Waxwing, a winter visitor* © Wayne Lynch

power dams and water storage facilities built upstream in the 1900s have solved the flooding problem.

According to hydrologic studies done by Alberta Environment, however, the dams upstream are a factor only for small to medium floods; they would have a negligible effect on large floods, which of course are the ones to worry about. The City of Calgary has been blessed by a meteorological fluke, which has in the last few decades seen intense flood-producing storms to the north and south, but not right over the foothills in the Bow River drainage. It is only a matter of time...

It appears, however, that the residences across the river are relatively safe: mapping done for the city suggests that the "1% flood" (a flood so large that it has a 1% chance of happening in any given year; in this case, intermediate in size between the 1932 and 1897 floods on the Bow) would not inundate any Montgomery residences. It would however inundate part of Shouldice Park and many residences in Bowness. The 1% flood theoretically would submerge the picnic areas of lower Edworthy Park and almost all of Lawrey Gardens, and extend southwest of the regional pathway and CPR tracks at points downstream of the Coulee and upstream of Lawrey Gardens.

Continue southeastward along the path. Where the trees begin to thin out, a little spur loop trail leads to a grassy prominence ten metres left (east) of the trail. Here, down the slope to the east, you overlook the roof of the Edworthy ranch house. To the east of the home is an artificial pond (out of sight) that serves to catch spring water and stop it from reaching the railway tracks. This is why the trail is called "Pond Look-Out Trail": in earlier days, before the trees grew so tall, the pond could be seen from this benchland.

It was spring water that Tom Edworthy used to irrigate his crops. An old sandstone reservoir warmed the water before it was channelled downhill to the

crops, probably through a wooden pipe. The reservoir still exists in this area, although fenced off for safety reasons. Also in this general vicinity but upslope and to the east, is one of the four Bow Bank quarries. It was from this quarry that the sandstone for the Calgary Malt and Brewery Company building was quarried.[13]

Fifteen metres beyond the grassy prominence, the trail forks. The right fork climbs up the scarp and eventually reaches the top of the upper plateau of Edworthy Park. Our route follows the left fork, which stays more or less level. This fork soon meets a constructed trail, that, to the right, also climbs to the upper plateau. We, however, take the left, downhill fork that proceeds 50 metres to a small stream which is crossed on a wooden bridge. In all likelihood, this was the source of Tom Edworthy's crop irrigation water.

The perennial stream originates from a spring near the top of the escarpment. As usual, groundwater is flowing through a layer of sandstone to its exit at the spring, and while in the ground is prevented from percolating farther down by a layer of shale. The chemistry of this spring was studied during a University of Calgary project. The water was found to contain, among other things, sodium and chloride concentrations suggestive of contamination by road salt, and high nitrate concentrations probably explained by a natural source of nitrate in the subsurface.

Here during the winter months, you may hear a whirring sound – it is the wingbeats of a thousand Bohemian Waxwings flying overhead. Look up and watch their flight. Sometimes you may see the entire flock suddenly falter or pause and then rapidly change direction. This sudden change of direction may be an evasive manoeuvre to escape from a bird of prey. Sometimes, it is because an individual has spotted the plentiful food supply of a European Mountain Ash tree laden with orange-red

ABOVE *Common Redpoll, a visitor from the sub-Arctic*
© Michael Buckley

berries. This tree grows in gardens in neighbouring communities and occasionally escapes into the near-pristine woods of the escarpment.

Here, also in winter, along this trail, you may see a flock of small birds with red caps. These are Common Redpolls, and, less frequently Hoary Redpolls. Redpolls migrate from the sub-Arctic, arriving in late October, returning to their northern homes in late April. Resembling a small sparrow, the male Redpoll develops a pink blush on its chest and rump before it departs – making it a most attractive sight.

Continue eastward along Pond Look-Out Trail. The trail passes through mixed woodland with Balsam and Aspen Poplars predominating and is beautiful in any season. In spring, it is bordered by Western Canada White Violets. The edge conditions between the prairie on the plateau above and the woods below provide an important habitat for birds. Look and listen for them. The careful observer will be well rewarded.

Ultimately you arrive at a small parking lot at the base of the slope. A road connects this parking lot with the main parking lot at the mouth of the Coulee, where this loop began.

Footnotes – Walk Two

[1]   Michael C. Wilson, *Once Upon a River: Archaeology and Geology of the Bow River Valley at Calgary, Alberta, Canada*, Archaeological Survey of Canada, Paper No. 114, National Museum of Man Mercury Series, p. 267.

[2]   John Acorn, *Bugs of Alberta*, p. 34.

[3]   *Ibid.* p. 38.

[4]   Recounted by Morris Barraclough in a conversation, July 2001.

[5]   Jill Clayton, *Brickburn. Part of Calgary's Heritage*, Calgary Parks and Recreation, Unpublished, August 1990, pp. 15-16.

[6]   Federation of Alberta Naturalists, *Op. Cit.*, p. 167.

[7]   *Ibid.*

[8]   *Ibid.* p. 86.

[9]   Calgary Field Naturalists' Society, *Nose Hill: A Popular Guide*, p. 112.

[10] *Ibid.*

[11] *Ibid.* p. 103.

[12] *Ibid.* p. 109.

[13] In conversation with George Edworthy Jr. Also in James Dempsey, *Op. Cit.*

EDWORTHY PARK
THE RIVERSIDE

WALK THREE

OVERVIEW

An easy walk on flat ground, this route starts at the Harry Boothman Bridge near the shelter belt and orchard planted by George Edworthy Sr. From there, it heads west along the Christmas Tree Trail adjacent to the river and the riverine forest of Balsam Poplars and Red-osier Dogwoods. Unlike the other walks, this route is not described as a loop.

BELOW *Gravel "bedload" of the Bow River near the Harry Boothman Bridge* © J. Osborn

The route begins at the south end of the Harry Boothman Bridge, which may be approached either from the parking lot on the north side of the bridge, or the parking lot at the bottom of Coulee Road accessed from Spruce Drive S.W.

The Harry Boothman Bridge is named in memory of Harry Boothman, Director of Parks for the City of Calgary. Harry and Hattie Boothman lived in the Edworthy ranch house for 14 years, from 1962 to 1976. Hattie was a key participant in the Calgary Field Naturalists' Society and contributed to writing a study of five natural areas in that Society's field guide.

Note the rounded cobbles along the river's edge, under the south end of the bridge. They will be well exposed in the fall but may be completely submerged in high early-summer flows. These cobbles are part of the river's "bedload", that sediment which is pushed and rolled along the bed of the river. Gravel of this size cannot be moved during normal low flows of the river, but may be moved during high spring runoffs, and certainly moves during flood events. Hence, this gravel can be said to be in temporary storage. Rocks that are supplied to river systems by landslides and debris flows tend to be very angular, but as the rocks at the bottom of a river roll, hop, and crack against each other, the corners and edges are beaten off, leaving them rounded as observed here. Another common product of river transport is sorting by sediment size or mass; notice that there is little or no sand, silt, or clay mixed in with the gravel here.

At the south end of the bridge, you will notice three large marker rocks of Porcupine Hills sandstone. These came from the Bow River when the footings for the bridge were excavated. Bill Robinson, a long-time employee of Parks and Recreation, suggested

that they be placed there instead of bollards. He recognized the beauty of these rocks. Look closely and you will notice that they are full of embedded fossilized shells. These are freshwater clams that lived in the river and pond systems that produced the Porcupine Hills Formation. Similar clam-laden rocks have been placed at the north end of the bridge.

Our route will proceed westward from these rocks, but first notice the large grassy rectangle containing a picnic area and children's playground, just south of the bridge. Many people have wondered about the lovely old trees – predominantly White Spruce and hybrid poplar that are clearly planted around the margins of a rectangle. A hedge of Caragana forms an outer "wall".

These trees were planted by George Edworthy Sr., son of Thomas Edworthy. In 1939, the Edworthy family planned to build a new farmhouse north of the tracks in this area. Much like today, there were problems with road access. The dirt track down the bottom of the Coulee washed out in the late 1930s, so George Edworthy and Hy Zeer built an alternate route they called "Big Road". This is the obvious steep track descending the east wall of the Coulee near its mouth.

The proposed solution to the access problems was to build a new house north of the tracks and a foot-bridge across the river. The plan included building a garage on the north side of the river. The Edworthy family would walk from their house to the car on the other side of the river, thereby circumventing the problems of icy winter access from the south side.

In anticipation of this move, George Edworthy Sr. planted 12,000 trees here and meticulously weeded them with help, in part, from Lou Zeer, Hy Zeer's son. The war, however, soon intervened and the house was never built.

Seen from the escarpment above, these trees resemble a large "shelterbelt". Settlers and pioneers used this term for trees that sheltered their homes from the wind – in

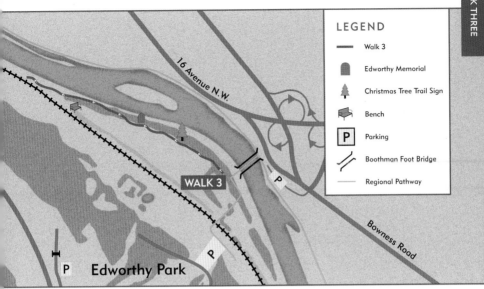

LEGEND

——	Walk 3
	Edworthy Memorial
	Christmas Tree Trail Sign
	Bench
P	Parking
	Boothman Foot Bridge
——	Regional Pathway

16 Avenue N. W.

WALK 3

Edworthy Park

Bowness Road

effect, a planted windbreak. As you drive through rural Alberta, you will see many shelterbelts that were planted years ago. Sometimes, as is the case just south of Red Deer, you may see vast rows of trees planted during the "Dirty Thirties" to help prevent topsoil from blowing off the fields.

Over the past 40 years, picnickers and other users have enjoyed the Edworthy shelterbelt. You will notice that within the rectangle there is a depression in the soil surrounded by a grassed earth berm. This is the old skating rink where neighbourhood children learned to skate. On a mild winter's day, the fire pits were used to provide refreshments of hot dogs and hot chocolate. A generation of children grew up enjoying skating here.

In the spruce trees of the shelterbelt, until about 1996, a pair of Great Horned Owls nested. Many people walked past the fledglings perched silently in the trees, without detecting their presence. They have not nested here in recent years – perhaps due to the installation nearby of a tall light standard by the Parks Department.

Now, walk westward from the clam rocks, on the river side of the planted spruce trees.

Beyond the rectangular shelterbelt and adjacent to Picnic Site #1A, you will notice many crabapple trees to your left. This is the orchard, planted also in 1939. During the days of the Shaganappi Ranch and later when Tom Edworthy's children and grandchildren lived here, fruit trees provided food for the family. At one time, a Horse Chestnut tree grew here.

A few hundred metres further west along this path, the trail becomes the "Christmas Tree Trail". As the sign indicates, this trail was surfaced in 1991 using 800 cubic metres of wood chips from 30,000 recycled Christmas trees. These chips were difficult to walk on for several years after they were laid as they were spongy and caused strain on the tendons. Today, this is easy walking. There is a grassy field to the left where a few hawthorn trees grow. To the right is a riverine forest with Red-osier Dogwood shrubs, and Balsam Poplar trees.

Along this section of the river, especially in August and September, you may be rewarded by the sight of dozens of migrant birds, especially flycatchers, warblers and sparrows. Members of the Calgary Field Naturalists' Society regularly see up to fifty species on an outing here.

Soon you will come to a large sandstone boulder with a brass plaque. This commemorates George Edworthy Sr. George became Western Division General Manager of the United Grain Growers. He was very active in the Calgary Stampede. George Edworthy Sr. kept a detailed diary and it is thanks to this habit that so much is known about the history of Edworthy Park. His manuscript of the history of Shaganappi Ranch is in the Glenbow Museum archives.

Just behind the sandstone memorial, in July, is a patch of white Canada Anemones. Continuing west, you encounter, to your left, a mostly open field dotted with some small spruce trees. Signs indicate that the small trees were planted by a Boy Scout troop. Further west are large poplars clearly planted in rows. This is an old tree nursery of the City of Calgary. A hawk is often perched high in one of these trees. Sometimes, as mentioned in the last chapter, it is a Swainson's Hawk; at other times, a Red-tailed Hawk.

When walking in this area, in a gap in the trees where you have a clear view of the river, watch for an Osprey swiftly dropping with a loud splash into the river, as it catches its fishy prey. Equally exciting is to see an Osprey flying off, grasping a fish in its talons.

Both Ospreys and Bald Eagles thrive in Edworthy Park. The fishing in this area is great. Near the Harry Boothman Bridge are spawning areas for Brown and Rainbow Trout, Suckers, Whitefish, Pike, etc. Fishers of all sorts enjoy this area – whether they are eagles, ospreys, kingfishers or humans!

It is also in this area – between the river and the pathway – that the irrigation ditches for the Shaganappi Ranch may still be found.

TOP LEFT George Edworthy Sr.
© Glenbow Archives NA-1494-34
***ABOVE** Bald Eagle soaring*
© Wayne Lynch
***LEFT** Osprey* © Wayne Lynch
***OPPOSITE LEFT** Tree Swallows may be seen in the riverine forest* © Wayne Lynch

Eventually, the path turns slightly left and then forks. Continue straight ahead on the right fork. Near this fork, in midsummer, you are treated to the sight of a beautiful white daisy. This is an Ox-Eye Daisy, introduced from Europe, which, although common elsewhere, seems uncommon in Edworthy Park.

Ahead of you is a bench, a great place to pause to watch the river and wait for Ospreys or other birds to come along. Yellow Warblers nest nearby. To the south is a wooded area. Near the end of this trail, you will find the old foundations of the Brickburn Post Office.

You may turn back anytime, returning to the starting point, enjoying what you may discover on your own. This is an enjoyable walk in the fall when the dogwood leaves have turned red, and the aspens are golden. The overall impact of the autumn leaves at their colourful prime is spectacular!

DOUGLAS FIR
TRAIL WEST

WALK FOUR

OVERVIEW

The Douglas Fir Trail traverses the high, steep Spruce Cliff/Wildwood escarpment. Our route climbs up a steep staircase to a lookout at Dead Man's Drop and then down another staircase and out to the major landslide area where the trail links up to the regional pathway. This is a north-facing escarpment with fragile native vegetation, and walkers are encouraged to stay on the main trail. Going off trail or around destroys the vegetation which may take years to regrow due to harsh conditions. Caution is required at the landslide area due to potential rockfall.

BELOW *Horsetails (Equisetum)* © E. Gilliam

From the main parking lot on the south side of the river, turn east on the paved Bow River regional pathway. Approximately 250-300m east, you arrive at the west entrance of the Douglas Fir Trail. A sandstone rock marker and city map-sign stand at the intersection.

Leaving the regional pathway, the trail heads for the base of the escarpment and almost immediately drops down into a long, shallow, linear depression. Such depressions exist in similar topographic situations farther east. They most likely are old channels of the Bow River, cut when the river was at a slightly higher level, and south of its present course.

Spring arrives with subtlety on the Douglas Fir Trail. At the first bend in the trail, near the base of the escarpment, one of the first plants to be seen in spring is horsetail (Equisetum). Here the spring water provides moisture required for horsetails to thrive. Among still-living genera, this is one of the oldest plants known. Equisetum originated back in the Devonian period, almost 400 million years ago, before seeds had evolved. Consequently, the plant's reproductive system is based on spores.

The Equisetum along the Douglas Fir Trail is approximately 30 centimetres tall. Settlers used this ancient plant to scour pots and pans because it contains silica. Native Canadians boiled it for a drink and used it for horse medicine.[1] Horsetails provide food for moose, bears and horses alike.

Horsetails do not have flowers. In addition to stems that look like "horse-tails", you may see a cone-like structure on the top of a stem of some of them. This cone is covered with "spore-bearing scales" and has "four small threads or 'elators' which ...throw the spore from its resting place on the cone".[2]

TOP Red-breasted Nuthatch © E. Gilliam
BOTTOM LEFT White-breasted Nuthatch © E. Gilliam
BOTTOM RIGHT Western Canada White Violet in May © Michael Buckley

There are two species growing here; the finer and more abundant one is Meadow Horsetail, the coarser one is Field Horsetail.

There is nothing subtle about the beauty of Western Canada White Violets further along the trail. Here, in late May and June, hundreds of them border the trail. The overwhelming beauty of the violets is one of our favourite sights. The leaves are a larval food of a beautiful fritillary butterfly. If, later in the season, you notice leaves riddled with holes, you may be witnessing evidence that the caterpillar has fed here.[3]

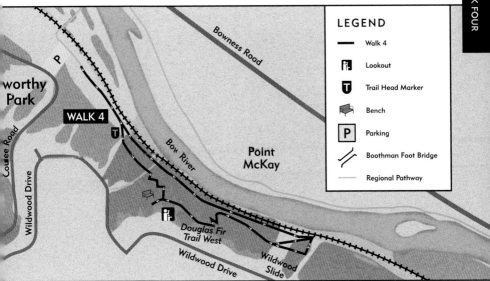

WALK 4

The trail climbs a short distance to Bridge 5122A, beneath which flows a small rivulet. This stream emanates from water seeping out of the ground at the little flat area about 40m up the slope. The groundwater probably is exiting from the bottom of a Porcupine Hills sandstone layer underneath the mud.

Approaching the bridge, you may see cavities made by nesting woodpeckers, nuthatches, and chickadees in the standing dead trees next to the trail. Many birds use standing dead trees – or "snags" – for nesting. This is especially obvious in early spring before the leaves are out.

Stand on the bridge and look for these nesting holes. You may hear the nasal "yank, yank" call of a Red-breasted Nuthatch. If you see a bird going head first down a tree, it is a nuthatch, the only North American bird to do so. This enables nuthatches to find insects missed by other birds, such as woodpeckers, which go up a tree. Nuthatches excavate holes in dead trees for their nests and smear the perimeter of the hole with pine or spruce resin.[4] Presumably, this tactic keeps out intruders such as squirrels and tree-climbing snakes.

In spring, you may hear a soft chatter between a breeding pair of nuthatches as they travel through the woods. Their nest may have four to seven white eggs speckled with reddish brown.[5] Although Red-breasted Nuthatches are the more common along the Douglas Fir Trail, it is possible that you may also see the larger White-breasted Nuthatch which favours the broad-leaved trees.

From this bridge, glance upwards at the old Balsam Poplar trees. Here in their canopy, you may see a flash of bright orange and hear a lyrical song. This is the Baltimore Oriole. The western end of the Douglas Fir Trail is a favourite habitat of the oriole and many migratory birds. It is a wonderful sight on a dreary rainy day – and of course in fair weather – to encounter a Baltimore Oriole. Perhaps, if you are lucky, you may detect its basket-like nest hanging from a tree branch – a masterpiece of weaving!

Balsam Poplars have sticky buds in the spring – their resin scents the air with a "spicy fragrance". In early spring, you may see birds – hungry from migration – eating their catkins. Annora Brown notes that "...a decoction of the resinous buds was sometimes successfully used by the Indians

TOP A Baltimore Oriole (male) © Wayne Lynch

MIDDLE Douglas-fir cone (with "mouse's tails") © Dave Elphinstone

BOTTOM White Spruce cones © O.F. Wachtler

in cases of snow-blindness but its application to the inflamed eye caused much pain".[6]

Natives held sacred such groves of poplar trees. The poplar "were the friends of the old people, while the children were taught not to harm the young saplings so that ... the trees and the children, might grow up together to be friends in their old age". Often old trees provided the "last resting place of a famous chief or the weary bones of a medicine woman..." [7].

Balsam Poplars are sometimes unfairly blamed for allergies. The fluffy seeds are airborne but allergists have indicated that the fluff is too large to be inhaled and unlikely to be the cause of allergies. It is more likely that the almost microscopic yellow pollen of spruce trees is to blame. Spruce pollen, virtually invisible except in years of heavy pollen production, is air-borne at the same time as Balsam Poplar fluff.

Beyond the bridge, we enter an area of White Spruce. The bark of the spruce is thin and rough. Its cones, under 5cm long, are narrow and cylindrically shaped with overlapping scales. If you "shake hands" (gently) with its needles, you will feel that the needles are sharp and stiff.

These features will distinguish it from the Douglas-fir which has soft, flat needles. Douglas-fir cones have overlapping scales at the bottom of which is a bract that "extends beyond the scale in three parts, almost like the back legs and tail of a hiding mouse"! [8] Douglas-fir's lower bark is corky and grooved; the upper is smooth with resin blisters. The lowest branches of a Douglas-fir tree, unlike the sweep of a spruce, are higher up. The thickness of the bark and the height of its lowest branches enable some Douglas-fir trees to survive fire.

About 75 metres beyond the high point of the first bridge, on the right, is the first Douglas-fir near the trail. It is about 50cm in diameter, with an eight cm stem growing out of it on the right. About three m beyond, on the left, (and about ten metres before the first railing), is a slightly smaller tree which a vandal has attacked with a hatchet. Resin is oozing over the injury, trying to protect it from infection.

The Douglas Fir Trail passes through one of the most easterly stands of Douglas-firs in Canada. Some of the trees here are at least 500 years old – pre-dating the arrival of Columbus in America. Because of drier conditions in Calgary, the Douglas-firs here are not as massive as those west of the Rockies.

In early June, you may see the lovely Purple Clematis, a vine climbing up shrubs and tree trunks. To quote Annora Brown again, "...its flowers, consisting of inconspicuous petals and four or five big blue sepals, look like lovely blue butterflies hovering amongst the greenery. One approaches them warily lest they should suddenly take wing".[9]

As you walk the trail, note that many trees lean in a downhill direction, apparently affected by the imperceptible downslope sediment movement called "creep". As well, sediment can be seen sloughing off below tree trunks in several places.

The trail soon descends and meets a short connector trail that serves as an exit downhill to the regional pathway. The junction is at the base of a coulee that has eroded headward into the crest of the Wildwood escarpment. A few metres upslope is the eroded watercourse that drains this coulee.

From the stream course, the Douglas Fir Trail continues eastward, climbing up stairs, and enters a grove of Douglas-fir trees. Here, again, are many Western Canada White Violets in June.

In recent years, a pair of Red-tailed Hawks nested in trees near here. Pause for a moment and you may see one of the hawks as it perches nearby or as it flies over in its search for food.

The trail crosses a relatively large V-shaped coulee bottom on Bridge 5122B. This is McMillan's Coulee, named after a Dominion land surveyor who had a sod house in the vicinity.[10] The coulee, about 350 m long, is the second-longest break in the escarpment, after the main Edworthy Park Coulee. The perennial creek continues to very slowly erode this coulee, but most of the erosion presumably occurred when flows were greater.

Another feature of the coulee is the riverine vegetation found at its south end, far removed from the river, one of the few places this occurs in Calgary.[11]

Just beyond this bridge, on the north side of the trail, in late spring, you may notice the pink buds or blue blossoms of Mertensia, also known as Lungwort. It is also found at the western entrance of the trail. The flowers of this plant change color after pollination. Beginning as "tightly furled pink buds", the buds turn blue as they expand.[12] Once the flowers are pollinated, the flowers turn pink again.

Some metres east of Bridge 5122B, the trail bends uphill and passes by a large sandstone outcrop. Cross-beds are obvious in the rock. This is an old sandstone quarry, one of the four quarries operated by Thomas Edworthy as part of his company, Bow Bank Quarries. This quarry was rented by Edworthy to the Canadian Pacific Railway. In exchange, the CPR built siding tracks to service Edworthy's quarries.

LEFT *Purple Clematis, "like butterflies"...* © L. McConnell

RIGHT *Mertensia Paniculata or Lungwort* © Michael Buckley

TOP *Police Car moth on Smooth Asters, August* © E. Gilliam
BOTTOM *Caterpillar of the Police Car Moth on Mertensia*
© Michael Buckley

At this quarry, small railway cars were loaded with sandstone. There was a cable and pulley system used to direct a loaded car downhill on a track. Gravity did the rest of the work. Meanwhile, an empty car was pulled uphill to the quarry – pulled by the downward force of the loaded car.

Sandstone from this quarry was carted across the frozen river one winter. It was used to build the home of Alfred Sidney McKay, a surveyor for the CPR and a leading citizen of early Calgary.[13] Built in 1903, McKay's house today is an historic site and is the clubhouse for the Point McKay community.

In spring, at the quarry, a few Star-flowered Solomon's-seal plants flower. As its name suggests, its dainty white blooms are star-shaped. Occasionally you may see a colony of these shade-loving plants which spread by suckers.

Continuing up the steps, on your right, note the stream running through McMillan's Coulee. This was ideal terrain for a buffalo jump with its proximity to a stream. In this general vicinity, bison bones have been found over the years. The buffalo jump may have predated the trees.

To the left (north), you will see the soft branches of *Juniperus horizontalis* as it creeps along the hillside. This juniper is very old as suggested by its size. At the first switchback of the trail, looking right (south), after late July, you will see some goldenrod plants. Their yellow shafts of flowers liven up the fall groundcover. Look carefully and you may notice that goldenrod grows in circular colonies. Dana Bush points out that:

All goldenrods within the circle are clones of one another, and are connected to each other by underground stems called rhizomes ...

If a goldenrod shoot comes up in a poor environment, the whole community will share in the misfortune, transferring toxins and nutrients back and forth through the rhizomes. The damaged plant will be fed and nurtured by the others... – a sort of floral socialism.[14]

Some people attribute allergies to goldenrod. It is not guilty, however, as the heavy pollen falls near the plant and does not become airborne. Like Balsam Poplars, this intriguing plant has been unfairly maligned. Near here, watch for the colourful Western Tanager with its red head and yellow breast; it has been seen here in June and July, and probably nests in the park. Ruby-crowned Kinglets sing throughout May and June as you pass by.

As you climb, the trail switchbacks again. As you near the lookout, note the huge Douglas-fir trees. Douglas-fir trees are a montane plant, a species found in the foothills and the mountain valleys. Here, at their base, however, we find prairie vegetation. White to deep-rose-coloured Cut-leaved Anemones bloom in June. This species is commonly called "windflower"

– indeed the word "anemone" is Greek for "wind"[15]. It usually grows in prairie settings. Seeds are produced with a cottony "fluff" which was burned by natives for its headache-curing smoke.[16] Other prairie plants found beneath the Douglas-fir trees include Harebells and Prairie Crocus. Here also is found Hairy Wild Rye grass. Enough sunshine penetrates the forest to sustain prairie wildflowers. Did the Douglas-fir trees come first or did the prairie vegetation grow first to be gradually supplanted by the trees?

Douglas-firs migrated down the Bow Valley from the Bow Summit area following the last glaciation. Pollen studies show that the trees had arrived in Bow Valley Provincial Park by 6,000 years ago and arrived in Calgary sometime after that.

The trail reaches the viewpoint known as the lookout. Neighbourhood children used to call this point "Dead Man's Drop", although not because of any particular unfortunate event. Earlier, in the 1930s and 1940s, the area was called "Bear Cliff" because bears were seen here.[17] In fact, they were seen in the area during the late 1950s and early 1960s. It is still possible to encounter Black Bears here during famine years when they follow the river valley eastward in search of food.

The expansive view from the lookout includes the three basic topographic levels of northwest Calgary. On the horizon is the highest level, the top of Nose Hill, a former

TOP LEFT *Fluffy seeds of the Cut-leaved Anemone* © Paul Beaulieu
TOP RIGHT *Goldenrod – well-loved by bumblebees* © E. Gilliam
BOTTOM *Gooseberry leaves in fall* © E. Gilliam

floodplain of the ancestral Bow River. The middle level supports the University of Calgary campus, Foothills Hospital, and, farther northwest, several residential communities including Varsity Acres and Silver Springs. This level is the top of ice-age sediments that partially filled the old valley that has cut into the upper level. The lower level is the floodplain that was created by post-glacial downcutting of the Bow River through the ice-age sediments. The community of Point McKay, just across the river, is built on this level. Shaganappi Trail and the Trans-Canada Highway can be seen climbing the inner Bow Valley slope between the lower and middle levels. Prominent on the far side in the river is a gravel bar that has been stabilized by vegetation. To the left, upriver, is the Harry Boothman Bridge.

To the west is seen the alluvial fan at the mouth of the Edworthy coulee, partly covered by the main parking lot. Nearby is the main picnic area with its shelterbelt of trees and shrubs.

Pausing for rest on the benches, you may hear one of the many chickadees that live in this forest. Although the most common species of chickadee observed is the Black-capped Chickadee, you might also, rarely, see a Mountain Chickadee. Similar in appearance at first glance, the Mountain Chickadee is distinguished by a white line or "eyebrow" over its eyes. In winter, chickadees vocalize their namesake song, "Chickadee-dee-dee". At the approach of spring, they sing a simple two-noted song, a "Feeee Beee" whistle. If you hear a chickadee which sounds raspy, look more closely. You might observe the uncommon Boreal Chickadee with its dark chocolate brown cap.[18] Even more rare is the Chestnut-backed Chickadee which has been observed in the park.

Near the Lookout, in spring and autumn, you may see many different species of

TOP *Mountain Chickadee* © Wayne Lynch
MIDDLE *Boreal Chickadee* © Wayne Lynch
BOTTOM *Black-capped Chickadee* © L. McConnell

migrating warblers as well as the tiny Ruby-crowned Kinglet. During the first week of May after a long winter, you may see a kinglet flitting among the branches searching for insects in the poplar catkins. At first, it may be observed in low bushes but, as the air temperature climbs and insects rise higher, it then frequents the uppermost branches of evergreens, where it nests. Listen for its lovely song ending with "cuppa tea, cuppa tea".

In fall and winter, Golden-crowned Kinglets search for insects at the ends of twigs. Often interspersed with chickadees, Golden-crowned Kinglets, like chickadees, are great acrobats. They undoubtedly appreciate seeds of the Black or Water Birches in other parts of the park.

In June, the Wolf Willow blooms. Its fragrance permeates the air on this section of the trail.

Just in front of the benches is a naturally occurring slab of sandstone. Look carefully and you may observe barely discernable ripple marks on its surface, consequences of the flowing water in which the original sand grains were deposited.

From the lookout benches, the trail leads directly upslope for 25 m to a junction. The left (easterly) fork is the continuation of the Douglas Fir Trail; however, go right to take another break at the bench on the westerly fork, where there is a magnificent view of the forested escarpment. In fall, to the right of the bench and downslope by four or so metres, there is a lovely combination of Smooth Asters, White Tufted Prairie Asters, and goldenrod. In spring, there are Prairie Crocuses. In June and July, you may see Common Yellow Paintbrush just down slope from the west end of the bench.

At the left end of the bench is a small patch of Kinnikinnick or Common Bearberry. The natives used this plant, with its glossy green, leathery leaves, as a tobacco substitute. In spring, it has tiny pink and white "urn-shaped" flowers. In autumn, "the shrub produces not

TOP *Ruby-crowned Kinglet in summer* © *Kathleen Roman*

BOTTOM LEFT *Golden-crowned Kinglet in winter* © *L. McConnell*

BOTTOM RIGHT *Buffaloberry* © *O.F. Wachtler*

only bright red berries but leaves brilliantly tinted and tipped with scarlet".[19]

Close to this bench, beyond the Kinnikinnick, is a shrub of Canada Buffaloberry. Its bright red berries, high in saponin (the active ingredient in soap), were used by natives to make a type of "ice cream" or drink.[20] They must have had a secret recipe (or used lots of honey) as buffaloberries eaten raw are bitter! Some natives claim that eating buffaloberries has a salutary effect on the circulatory system – yet another clue to be researched by ethnobotanists.

As a City employee, Bill Robinson was responsible for building the original Douglas Fir Trail in the early 1970s. He stated that in the 1950s and 1960s, there were eagle pits in

the vicinity of the lookout. These pits were depressions dug in the ground, covered with vegetation. Carrion was placed on top of the vegetation to bait the eagles. When an eagle landed to feed, a native, concealed below, would reach up to capture it, to pluck a tail feather. These feathers were highly prized for ceremonial and sacred purposes.

The forest here blends into mixed aspen woodland. Aspen Poplar is the dominant species. Here in spring, watch for a large chocolate brown butterfly with wings edged in cream. Look more closely and you will see a row of beautiful blue spots. This is the Mourning Cloak butterfly. It hibernates in hollow trees or brush-piles and other crevices. In spring, it is often the first butterfly to fly because it has spent the winter as an adult. The row of blue spots may fool predators – mostly birds – into attacking the edge of the wings instead of the butterfly's head. You may also see a Mourning Cloak in late July: this is the second generation of butterflies.[21]

Shortly after the Mourning Cloak appears in spring, you may observe large orange butterflies. These are the anglewings, including Satyr Anglewing, Green Commas and Grey Commas. The anglewings are distinctive – the edges of their wings are deeply cut out and sharply defined, almost like lace. Both Mourning Cloaks and Satyr Anglewings (which also overwinter as adults) like the sap that oozes from trees such as aspens or willows in early spring.

Here, too, in recent years, a Compton's Tortoise Shell butterfly has been observed. Although at first glance it appears to be an anglewing, as its background colour is orange with black, its wings are more rounded on the bottom edge. From nearby, given the correct vantage point, you may observe a white spot on its wings. Like the

TOP *Satyr Anglewing butterfly* © *L. McConnell*
UPPER MIDDLE *Canadian Tiger Swallowtail butterfly* © *L. McConnell*
LOWER MIDDLE *Mourning Cloak butterfly* © *L. McConnell*
BOTTOM *Compton's Tortoise Shell butterfly* © *L. McConnell*

Mourning Cloak and the anglewings, it too enjoys sap from trees and may be observed on an Aspen Poplar in April. It is a rare sight.

In May and June, the transition zone between aspen forest and prairie is the favourite habitat of the Tiger Swallowtail butterfly. It is thought that the long tail is actually a survival adaptation, as the hind edge with its eyespots and pointed tail seen in side profile look like the head, antennae and eyes of the butterfly.[22] This is called "back to front mimicry".[23] A bird trying to catch this end of the butterfly would be left with non-essential tail in its beak as the butterfly flies away.

The food sources of swallowtails include chokecherries, willows and aspens. All three of these plants are found in this area. Aspens, especially those on the edge of a cliff or on the top of a hillside, provide strategic lookouts for the butterflies. Perched in the treetops, the male swallowtail can keep a lookout for females in its territory.[24]

In late August, you may be fortunate enough to come across the caterpillar of a swallowtail. One observed nearby was large with a deep chocolate brown as its background colour. A tiny head, at its front, was obscured by a large false head. Here two false eyespots – blue circled by yellow – were situated to deceive predators. An orange line separated this false head from its thorax. Blue spots were found along its sides. It was in its wandering stage, searching for a suitable pupating site. Within two days, it had changed from caterpillar to pupa, suspending itself by a girdle of silk around a twig. This silk girdle is characteristic of swallowtail pupa. The pupa itself looked like a dried-brown, rolled-up aspen leaf with green edges. Eventually, in May or June, the adult butterfly emerges from the pupa. Shortly after, it will be high in the treetops, or sailing above open spaces.

Also in this area, relics from a nearby farm have been observed, notably, some draft horse bones, old containers, and other items in an old farm dump.

Backtrack downhill to the junction where the Douglas Fir Trail continues eastward (right), traversing the upper part of the escarpment. This sunny stretch of the trail is beautiful in the autumn. On the right (south) side of the trail, notice a showy clump of Hedysarum alpinum in June and July. It is a member of the Pea Family which fixes nitrogen into the soil. It has bacteria nodules on its roots which take "unusable nitrogen from the air and converts it into a form [that plants] can use".[25]

Soon, to the right of the trail, small pink daisy-like flowers are seen in the fall. These are pink fleabanes. They are a composite flower, with many rays of flowers. Here is one of the best locations in the park to observe this fleabane.

The fall colours along this section of the trail are brilliant. The cotoneaster bushes, flaming red, are non-native, but have been seeded by birds from plants in the neighbouring community. Here, from October through the winter, you may see a flock of Pine Grosbeaks eating the cotoneaster berries or other seeds. The female grosbeak is a dull grey with a burnished orange head and rump. The male is spectacular with its red breast and head. Its thick beak, (hence the name "grosbeak"), is highly suited for eating berries and large seeds.[26]

Often seen along this portion of the trail are Red-shafted or Yellow-shafted Flickers,

LEFT Swallowtail Pupa hanging by a thread © L. McConnell

RIGHT Swallowtail Caterpillar © Marie Maitland

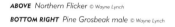

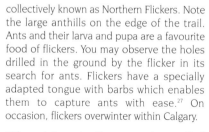

ABOVE Northern Flicker © Wayne Lynch

BOTTOM RIGHT Pine Grosbeak male © Wayne Lynch

TOP LEFT Pink Fleabane © E. Gilliam

TOP RIGHT Hedysarum alpinum © Paul Beaulieu

collectively known as Northern Flickers. Note the large anthills on the edge of the trail. Ants and their larva and pupa are a favourite food of flickers. You may observe the holes drilled in the ground by the flicker in its search for ants. Flickers have a specially adapted tongue with barbs which enables them to capture ants with ease.[27] On occasion, flickers overwinter within Calgary.

Other visitors to these woods are Red Crossbills and White-winged Crossbills. These are "peripatetic" birds. The term means that they wander in search of abundant cone crops. The upper and lower mandibles cross over each other, an adaptation for twisting open tree cones to extract seeds. If, as you walk along the trail, you notice fragments of cones floating in the air, look closely: in the trees, you may discover a flock of crossbills.

The male Red Crossbill is brick red; the female is "yellowish grey with a yellow rump". The White-winged Crossbill is a bright rosy red, similar to the Red Crossbill,

but has white wing bars. Crossbills are smaller than grosbeaks. They are members of the Finch Family and, like other finches, may hang upside down on tree branches in their search for food.[28]

Seeing a flock of crossbills is one of the delights of a walk along this part of the Douglas Fir Trail! Although you are most likely to observe them in fall, you may encounter crossbills at any time of the year. Both species nest in any month of the year, when cones are abundant, usually high in conifer trees. During the winter of 2001-2002, a large flock of White-winged Crossbills was observed for several months on this upper portion of the Douglas Fir Trail.

As you continue east along the trail, you will see a small grove of Common Chokecherry bushes mixed with Saskatoons. The Saskatoons bloom in May and are followed in early June by chokecherries. Saskatoons have a cluster of white blooms. Although chokecherries have similar blooms, their flowers are distinguished from Saskatoons

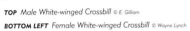

TOP *Male White-winged Crossbill* © E. Gilliam
BOTTOM LEFT *Female White-winged Crossbill* © Wayne Lynch

ABOVE *Chokecherry in bloom* © O.F. Wachtler
BOTTOM RIGHT *Saskatoon blossoms* © M. Bailey

by the long finger-like cluster with prominent stamens and yellowish colour. Differences in blooming time and the leaves of each plant confirm the identification.

Please leave the berries as migratory birds depend on them. Chokecherries have a form of cyanide in their leaves, seeds and bark that is poisonous. For this reason, chokecherry wood smoke should never be inhaled nor should leaves or other poisonous parts be eaten.

As you walk along the trail, you may feel dwarfed by the tall Douglas-fir and White Spruce trees. Look closely, though, and just before the railings resume, you will also see nature in miniature. Here on the bark of the Douglas-fir tree, you may see many different types of lichens. Lichens are a partnership between a fungus and an alga which mutually live together. Lichens grow slowly over centuries and are a sensitive indicator of air pollution. In polluted conditions, the great diversity of lichens is lost and fewer species grow.

In the mossy bank along the trail, many types of fungus may be observed. Here are tiny mushrooms along with a species resembling coral. Here we also see liverworts which have thrived on the earth's surface for 390 million years from the Devonian Period. Even the moss itself is intriguing especially viewed through a hand-held magnifying glass.

In the north-facing moss, notice a thirty cm tall plant with leaves that superficially resemble those of Saskatoons. A closer look reveals that its leaves are more elongated and more deeply serrated than those of Saskatoons. You have found the only known examples, over a six m long segment of trail, of Birch-leaved Spiraea (or White Meadowsweet), in Edworthy Park. From early to late August, the white blossoms appear – a late-blooming treat for the hiker along the trail. This plant is usually found in mountains and foothills, in cliff areas.[29] Here is an example of a species that could be totally destroyed in Edworthy by careless trampling.

TOP Birch-leaved Spirea (White Meadowsweet) © E. Gilliam

LEFT Snowberry in fall – plentiful along the Douglas Fir Trail © E. Gilliam

RIGHT One-sided Wintergreen © O.F. Wachtler

Continue to Bridge 5122C. Because of soil slumping, many patches of "drunken forest" exist east of the Lookout, but around this bridge the trees are particularly "inebriated". Part of the reason is the numerous seeps above, below, and adjacent to both ends of the bridge, which destabilize the ground. Immediately above each end of the bridge is a shallow depression a few metres across, created by sapping of surface sediment by the seeping water.

In winter, ice from these seeps pushes against the bridge, making it an engineering challenge to keep the bridge on the slope. The shadiness makes rehabilitating the undergrowth another challenge, and vegetation at both ends of the bridge has been trampled by walkers trying to avoid ice flows. The springwaters collect in a

rather messy-looking gully below the bridge, and more springs farther down contribute to a perennial stream that is one of the largest on the escarpment. The City has attempted to divert this water underneath the regional pathway and CPR tracks by means of a vertical drain whose corrugated sheet-metal cylinder can be seen well below the bridge. Much water still reaches the pathway however.

The trail now descends the escarpment by means of a switchbacking stairway. Near the bottom of the stairway is a large Douglas-fir tree that has been cored by the City of Calgary; tree rings indicate an age of over 500 years.[30]

The 4th bridge, 5122D, crosses a stream course that is usually dry only because the stream is intercepted by another city-installed vertical drain just upslope from the bridge. Conditions are still moist here, particularly in spring, so willows are common. The catkins of willows, Trembling Aspen and Balsam Poplars are an early source of food for migrating birds and for overwintering species such as chickadees.

Next to the bridge are many Field Horsetails. Pink Wintergreen blooms here in July. Called "wintergreen" because its leaves are evergreen, its flowers are especially lovely with their pink, fragrant petals. Annora Brown comments, "The leaves were believed to have a healing effect on bruises and so were used for shin plasters".[31] There is good reason why this might have been the case. The leaves of wintergreen contain salicylic acid, the active ingredient in aspirin. Indeed, salicylic acid was originally isolated from the bark of willows, which are in the genus Salix.

Just beyond the boardwalk, in early summer, you may see the native Blue Columbine. This blue and white flower adds colour to the shady woods. Scotter and Flygare describe the flowers with their bluish spurs as making "...a fanciful resemblance to doves perched and facing inward around a drinking dish, the wings being represented by the sepals".[32] Indeed, the name "columbine" refers to Columba, the Dove.

An erosional washout can be seen upslope of the trail, just east of the boardwalk that extends from the east end of the bridge. A small steep scarp is bordered by trees with increasingly exposed roots. The brown and dark grey horizons exposed in the small scarp are shale beds of the Porcupine Hills Formation.

Perhaps as you continue along the trail you may see a Downy Woodpecker as it searches for insects. Including flickers, there are four types of woodpeckers you are likely to see in Edworthy Park. The first two are common – the Downy Woodpecker and the larger Hairy Woodpecker. If it has a red patch on the back of its head, it is a male. The Downy Woodpecker can be distinguished from the Hairy "by its smaller size, short stubby bill, and black spots on white outer [tail] feathers".[33] The Atlas of Breeding Birds of Alberta further states: "Like many other woodpeckers, it searches for wood-boring beetle larvae, chipping away at a tree to reach the insect's tunnel, then impaling the occupant on its barbed tongue. Other insects are sought on the tree bark and in crevices".[34] The Hairy Woodpecker is "larger, has a much longer bill and, in most cases, has white outer tail feathers".[35] It is less common along the Douglas Fir Trail.

TOP Downy Woodpecker (male) © E. Jones
BOTTOM Hairy Woodpecker (female) © Wayne Lynch

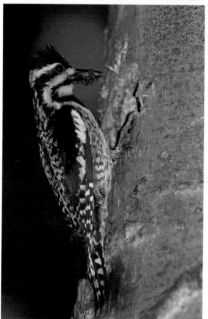

Farther along, you may see spruce or Douglas-fir trees with the bark removed. This is the work of the Three-toed Woodpecker which strips the bark off dead or dying trees in search of insects. It is a rare treat to see one of these quiet birds in winter along the Douglas Fir Trail. Other woodpeckers have four toes but this woodpecker has only three. The male has a yellow crown, so is unmistakable. Even if you do not see a Three-toed Woodpecker, you may nevertheless hear its distinctive drumming.[36]

Three other species of woodpecker are rarely seen. It is possible that the crow-sized Pileated Woodpecker may visit the park occasionally. In addition, a Black-backed Woodpecker has been seen. On a spring day, you may see a Yellow-bellied Sapsucker as it drills rows of holes, usually in dying trees, to extract sap. In the aspen woods bordering this upper portion of the Douglas Fir Trail, we have seen a Yellow-bellied Sapsucker being followed by a Ruby-throated Hummingbird which undoubtedly was opportunistically waiting for the sap to flow. In the park, you may also see two other species of hummingbird – the Rufous and the Calliope.

The Douglas Fir Trail passes through a forest of White Spruce and Douglas-firs where you may see a small, elusive bird with its downward curved beak. Watch as the Brown Creeper starts its hunt for insects from the base of one tree, spirals upward and then flies to another tree where it repeats this process. When the creeper perceives danger, it flattens itself against the bark of a spruce or aspen tree and is scarcely noticeable with the camouflage provided by its brown and white colouration.

The trail ultimately arrives at the large bare portion of the slope known as the Wildwood Slide. This is the site of the most significant landsliding to have occurred on the escarpment. Large sandstone blocks included in finer sediment in the lower part of the slope suggested to investigators in the middle 20th Century that a large failure incorporating the Porcupine Hills bedrock had occurred some time earlier. In the 1950s and

TOP Three-toed Woodpecker (male) © Wayne Lynch
BOTTOM Yellow-bellied Sapsucker © Wayne Lynch

1960s the lower edge of the landslide debris at the base of the slope occasionally would move over the CPR tracks, and mudflows emanating from the debris sporadically would cover the tracks. Meanwhile, ice would build up on the tracks in winter as water from the springs on the slide face would freeze. There was plenty of work for CPR maintenance crews.

In 1971, movement of the unstable mass at the bottom of the slope accelerated and the City of Calgary initiated an engineering study. The main culprit implicated in the continued creep of the landslide debris was the water running down from springs in the bare slope above. The engineers working on this study thought that this spring activity was exacerbated by lawn-watering and leaky pipes related to the residential development that took place on the flats above the escarpment in the 1950s. In any event, the major rehabilitation measure was installation of a network of perforated drainage pipes in the subsurface of the lower slope, whose purpose is to keep the groundwater table low. A surface drain was installed at the base of the bare slope to capture water of the major spring and pipe it to the river. Final landscaping of the lower slope was finished in 1977. The efforts appear to have been generally successful, although measurements in the early 1990s showed that the landslide mass was still creeping forward several mm per year.

The Douglas Fir Trail separates the barren landslide scar above from the gentler, engineered slope below. At the top of the landslide scar, a few metres of gravel overlies a vertical cliff of fractured Porcupine Hills sandstone. Below the vertical cliff is a slope of alternating shale and sandstone, much of it covered by mud and rocks washed down from above. The major spring in the slide area emanates from the base of the sandstone cliff; groundwater runs along the top of the shale, through the sandstone, to feed the spring. The water is collected in the large drain surrounded by the obvious wired-down gravel berm near the trail. The drain

TOP *Brown Creeper* © E. Gilliam

BOTTOM *Ice flow and "drunken" trees* © Sean Jackson

passes underneath the regional pathway and CPR tracks and empties into the river. Concrete highway dividers aligned parallel to the chain-link fence are designed to stop falling/rolling rocks from crossing the trail.

The Douglas Fir Trail continues eastward past the slide and descends steps to a point near the bottom of the escarpment, where a connector trail from the regional pathway meets the Douglas Fir Trail. Walkers may want to continue eastward on the Douglas Fir Trail, but the loop we describe here descends to the regional pathway, and returns on that pathway to the starting point. One may also descend to the regional pathway via the switchbacking dirt road on the lower, engineered part of the Wildwood Slide.

Walking westward on the regional pathway, observe the small streams of water, generated by the springs passed on the Douglas Fir Trail, reaching the bottom of the slope. Most of this water is effectively diverted underneath the pathway in summer, but in winter, the still-seeping water forms ice both on the slope and on the pathway.

On the return along the regional pathway, one also passes a pair of benches with a sandstone boulder in between. In 1999, the original bench at this site was struck by said boulder after it acquired considerable kinetic energy during its roll down the slope. The bench sacrificed itself to keep the boulder from crossing the pathway.

TOP *Rufous Hummingbird (male)* © Wayne Lynch
BOTTOM *Rufous Hummingbird (male)* © Wayne Lynch

ABOVE *Rufous Hummingbird (male) with sun highlighting its gorget* © Wayne Lynch

Footnotes – Walk Four

[1]   Annora Brown, *Old Man's Garden*, p. 139.

[2]   *Ibid.*

[3]   C.D. Bird et al., *Alberta Butterflies*, p. 250.

[4]   Federation of Alberta Naturalists, *The Atlas of Breeding Birds of Alberta*, p. 210.

[5]   *Ibid.*

[6]   Annora Brown, *Op. Cit.*, pp. 249-251.

[7]   *Ibid.* p. 251.

[8]   "Edworthy Park Natural Areas", a pamphlet produced by Calgary Parks & Recreation, Natural History Services.

[9]   Annora Brown, *Op. Cit.*, p. 90.

[10]   Before McMillan could prove up his homestead, he died and the land was bought by Tom Edworthy. George Edworthy Sr., "Edworthy Family History, Early History of Calgary, Wildwood", p. 1.

[11]   The other notable place is Paskapoo Slopes where riverine vegetation grows upslope far removed from the river.

[12]   C. Dana Bush explains the chemical process whereby the tight pink buds unfurl, carbon dioxide is released, the cell sap becomes alkaline and the blooms turn blue. Once pollinated, the flowers turn pink again, *Op. Cit.*, p. 48.

[13]   City of Calgary, Parks/Recreation Department, Natural History Services, "Resource Package for Edworthy Park Area", p. 31.

[14]   C. Dana Bush, *Op. Cit.*, p. 48.

[15]   Annora Brown, *Op. Cit.*, p. 12.

[16]   *Ibid.* p. 91.

[17]   In conversation with Roland Showalter, whose family lived in a sandstone house near what is now Shaganappi Library.

[18]   Federation of Alberta Naturalists, *Op. Cit.*, pp. 207-209.

[19]   Annora Brown, *Op. Cit.*, p. 225.

[20]   George W. Scotter and Hälle Flygare, *Wildflowers of the Canadian Rockies*, p. 74.

[21]   C.D. Bird et al., *Alberta Butterflies*, p. 216.

[22]   John Feltwell, *The Natural History of Butterflies*, pp. 54-55.

[23]   *Ibid.*

[24]   C.D. Bird et al., *Op. Cit.*, p. 106.

[25]   C. Dana Bush, *Op. Cit.*, p. 34.

[26]   Federation of Alberta Naturalists, *Op. Cit.*, p. 308.

[27]   *Ibid.* p. 175.

[28]   *Ibid.* pp. 312-313.

[29]   George Scotter and Halle Flygare, *Op. Cit.*, p. 58.

[30]   Bill Robinson, long-time employee of the City of Calgary, Parks and Recreation Department, now retired, cored this tree.

[31]   Annora Brown, *Op. Cit.*, p. 167.

[32]   Scotter and Flygare, *Op. Cit.*, p. 154.

[33]   Federation of Alberta Naturalists, *Op. Cit.*, pp. 171-172.

[34]   *Ibid.* p. 171.

[35]   *Ibid.* p. 172.

[36]   *Ibid.* p. 173.

QUARRY ROAD TRAIL, LAWREY GARDENS & DOUGLAS FIR TRAIL EAST

WALK FIVE

OVERVIEW

This relatively long route begins on Quarry Road Trail. A wealth of wildflowers, including some very uncommon plants, is seen here. In spring, every step of the way, you are accompanied by the lyrical music of songbirds. The route passes through an area of sandstone quarries, crosses the railroad track at a level crossing, and then doubles back westward, in part along the regional pathway. Passing a cove of the Bow River, and Willow Pond with its frog population, the route ultimately goes back across the tracks. Two alternatives are offered to return to the start – parallel to the tracks with a stop at South Sora Pond, or up the stairs and east along the Douglas Fir Trail.

BELOW Red-tailed Hawk © Wayne Lynch

STARTING POINT:

Park in the parking lot at the end of the little gravel road off the southeast end of Cedar Crescent, just beyond the intersection of Cedar Crescent and Spruce Drive S.W. Beware of high-speed bicyclists, especially on the downhill portion of Quarry Road Trail.

Quarry Road Trail was built in 1927 by Bill Hilton.[1] Hilton was the caretaker at Tregillus's Rosscarrock Ranch. His family lived in the ranch house, an old brick house south of Bow Trail and 37th Street at about 4th Avenue S.W. This lovely red-brick house was demolished in the 1960s. According to Hilton's niece, Shirley, it is unclear why Quarry Road was built. One may speculate that it was for transporting sandstone down the hillside to the CPR tracks — however, this was after the period when sandstone was the main building material of the town. Another reason may have been to provide access for squatters and residents of Lawrey Gardens. Yet another possibility was that it was designed to transport hay and other crops up the slope from Lawrey Gardens. A short segment of the upper portion was relocated to accommodate an expansion of Shaganappi Golf Course in the 1990s.

Walk down the gravelled Quarry Road Trail and after 100 m or so, pass the Douglas Fir Trail intersection on the left. Keep to the right, along the chain link fence. Here you see the expanded Shaganappi Golf Course. Originally, it was Calgary's first cemetery. The location was unsuitable because the sandstone beneath made grave digging difficult. Ultimately, the graves were moved to Union Cemetery. By 1915, it had become the site of Shaganappi Golf Course. Much of the land was given to the City by the Federal Government for use as a park.

TOP *Buffalo Bean* © E. Gilliam
BOTTOM LEFT *Shooting Star* © Wayne Lynch
BOTTOM RIGHT *Early Coralroot* © L. McConnell

The eastern end of the golf course was part of the Jackson Ranch. The low-lying land was home to Jackson's Pond. Many Calgarians enjoyed tobogganing down Jackson Coulee where Bow Trail now runs east of 26th Street S.W. Charlie Jackson was Calgary's first milkman. He and his brother Tom owned much of the land in what was then west Calgary. With W.J. Tregillus, Charlie Jackson was involved in importing fine Holstein cattle from abroad.[2]

The trail passes into mixed woodland. This is an important habitat for migratory birds. In response to community concerns to preserve this valuable habitat, the back nine

LEGEND

———	Walk 5
- - -	Other Route
(A)	Alternate Route A
(B)	Alternate Route B
🪑	Bench
P	Parking
———	Regional Pathway

South Sora Pond

Parkdale

Lawrey Gardens

Douglas Fir Trail East

Spruce Bank Crescent

Willow Pond

Cedar Crescent

Spruce Drive

37 Street S.W.

orial Dr. N.W.

WALK 5

P

Quarry Road Trail

of the redone Shaganappi Golf Course was constructed to preserve the dryland willow bushes and mature Balsam Poplars, and was reseeded with native grasses. This helped preserve the natural habitat to the greatest extent possible. Today, as before, the back nine is a regular hunting ground for a pair of Red-tailed Hawks – often, they are circling overhead, hovering to spot some prey and then dropping down to capture it. Coyotes frequent the 16th hole's putting green.

The rising air currents along this portion of the river valley are highly favourable for the soaring of hawks and eagles. Here sometimes in late fall and early spring you may see Bald Eagles soaring down the river valley.

Along this upper stretch of Quarry Road Trail grows a great variety of wildflowers. On a walk in late May, there is a profusion of Buffalo Beans, Star-flowered Solomon's-seals, Early Blue Violets, Early Coralroot, Western Canada White Violets, Common Chokecherries, Saskatoons, and False Solomon's-seals, to name a few.

Here, too, in early spring (mid-May to June), are shooting stars. The scientific name for

ABOVE *Red-tailed Hawk, Harlan's variety* © Wayne Lynch

LEFT *Striped Coralroot* © O.F. Wachtler
TOP RIGHT *Blunt-leaved Sandwort* © Gillean Daffern
BOTTOM RIGHT *Spotted Coralroot* © O.F. Wachtler

Wild Bergamot leaf and then smell your fingers – you will notice the oily, mint fragrance. A prized flower of hummingbirds and butterflies, it was also used as native medicine in sweat lodges to cure a muscle affliction.[5] Although called "Bergamot", it is not related to or the same as "Oil of Bergamot", an ingredient in Earl Grey tea which is the oil of a type of orange.

Follow the trail along the fence on the right until it bends to the left. Here there is a spectacular view of downtown Calgary. On the fence side of the path are some small plants with yellow stems and tiny white flowers which look like miniature orchid lips. Yes, these are orchids, but with a difference! They are *Corallorhiza trifida* – Early or Pale Coralroot. Its name refers to its underground rhizomes – characterized by coral-like interweaving branches[6]. This plant does not have a green stem because it lacks chlorophyll – it is a saprophytic plant which lives on decomposing organic matter.

Other, showier species of the same genus found here and on Lawrey Gardens include Striped and Spotted Coralroot.

Just after the trail switchbacks to the left under the power line, you might see a small Bracted Green Orchid. With its nondescript greenish yellow blooms, it seems to be misplaced in this area of woodland plants. We speculate that it favours this location because of moisture running off the trail. It lacks the large blooms usually associated with orchids. This orchid relies almost exclusively on male mosquitoes for their pollination, a useful purpose for this insect!

In the same vicinity, you may find the Blunt-leaved Sandwort. Wild Sarsparilla, locally rare, grows nearby.

Along the straightaway following the switchback, dark grey prairie soil can be seen overlying unweathered, tan-coloured sediment in the low trail-cuts on the left. The sediment contains flakes of Porcupine Hills sandstone and is probably slopewash.

this beautiful flower is *Dodecatheon*, Greek for twelve (*dode*) gods (*theos*), so named by the great botanist Linnaeus "because of a fancied resemblance to twelve gods at the Olympian gathering".[3] Shooting stars have other common names, including fish hook and bird bill.[4] Early in its blooming, the lovely deep-rose-coloured flower hangs its head. As it matures and turns into a seed pod, it points upwards to the sky. The basal leaves are a favourite food of wildlife. If the leaves survive, they disappear on their own after the flower has gone to seed; there will be no trace of the plant and you will have to wait until next spring to see it again.

Later in the summer, along this section of the trail, you may see Wild Bergamot, blooming prolifically. Also called *Monarda*, this flower is a member of the Mint family. Gently rub a

Shortly before the next switchback to the right, there is a path uphill to the left to a quarry with outcrops of sandstone on the sides and back wall. Excellent examples of cross-bedding can be observed in the outcrop at the switchback itself.

This is one of the many quarries after which the trail is named. Who owned and operated these quarries is unknown. What is known is that some of the sandstone from this area was used to build government buildings in Regina. A quarry called "Shaganappi Quarry" is referred to in an early newspaper article as the supplier of the sandstone for the Government Building in Regina. Further reference to the sandstone quarries along the Shaganappi escarpment can be found in the August 27, 1885 issue of *The Regina Leader Post* which describes a Mr. Geo. Melvin as "the discoverer of a fine sandstone quarry on the C.P.R., four miles west of Calgary".[7] Two weeks earlier, the same newspaper described a shipment of sandstone which arrived in Regina:

A carload of window-sill slabs arrived here on Friday for the new post-office and gaol. The slabs are taken from a fine freestone quarry about five miles west of Calgary by the C.P.C.[sic.] they are prepared and hewn before shipment and measure from three to five feet in length with a brehdth[sic.] and thickness of 12 x 8.[8]

Like the west end of Edworthy Park, Shaganappi Slopes was known for its sandstone. As you walk down Quarry Road Trail, a watchful eye will reward you with the old cuts made by the quarry operations on either side of the road.

At the second switchback are two park benches. Pause a moment and you will be rewarded by birdsongs from the Yellow Warblers which nest in this area. Some rare bird sightings have been made in this vicinity, including the Spotted Towhee. Avoiding densely forested areas, the towhee is "usually seen on or near the ground in dense, brushy cover and commonly frequents the shrubbery along prairie coulees,

TOP Great Horned Owl © Wayne Lynch
BOTTOM Barred Owl © Wayne Lynch

LEFT *False Solomon's-seals* © O.F. Wachtler

RIGHT *Early Blue Violet* © E. Gilliam

TOP *Red-osier Dogwood* © O.F. Wachtler

MIDDLE *Fairy Bells* © E. Gilliam

BOTTOM LEFT *Fairy Bell berries* © O.F. Wachtler

Great Horned Owl. In the winter months, on many occasions, the silhouette of a Great Horned Owl has been seen in trees and on the rooftops along Cedar Crescent. With its unmistakable ear tufts and large size, the Great Horned Owl is very impressive.[10] It mainly feeds on snowshoe hares and rodents.

Beyond the second switchback, the autumn colours of the Balsam Poplar and Trembling Aspen trees are spectacular. Vibrant yellows of the poplars mix with the brilliant red of Red-osier Dogwood leaves and are set against a green backdrop of spruce and Douglas-fir trees.

Described as one of the "beauties of the woodland at any time of the year" by Annora Brown, the Red-osier Dogwood has clusters of snow-white berries which contrast against the red of its leaves. Its bitter bark was dried in the sun or over fire and used by natives as a form of tobacco.[11] In winter, its red bark stands in sharp contrast to the snow. Its red branches were also used by the natives to weave baskets.

In spring, the trail is bordered by wildflowers. At the edge of the Balsam Poplars are the blooms of Common Chokecherries, Saskatoons, and dog-woods. Keep a watchful eye to the right (the upslope of the trail). Here, beyond the

streams, rivers, the tangles at forest edges and the undergrowth of open woodland". It has "black, white and chestnut underparts, a sparrow-like bill, a long tail, and a red iris".[9] It may pass through this area as a migrant, but it nests along Coulee Road in the western part of the park.

A Barred Owl has been seen in this area in recent years, even though its normal habitat is the foothills northwest of Calgary. More commonly seen in this area is the switchback and before the railing on the left where there is a bench, is an isolated patch of False Solomon's-seals with large green leaves with deeply-etched veins. The long stalks gracefully arch towards the trail and end in a long cylindrical cluster of tiny white flowers. This is one of the few places in the park and in the City of Calgary where you can see this plant. In the fall, the flowers have turned into deep red berries with purple spots.

Here also you can see (and perhaps hear?) Fairy Bells with its pairs of cream-coloured flowers in late spring. The autumn woods are clothed in colour including the almost fluorescent reddish-orange of the odd-shaped berries of this plant.

The large leaves along the trail edge in June belong to Cow Parsnip. In July, a flowering stem will reach over one metre in height. The flat-topped umbel will release a pleasant perfume, attractive to many insects too.

In May, Quarry Road Trail is graced at intervals by tiny Early Blue Violets. This is one of the first flowers to bloom in the spring and can be seen in a variety of habitats – at the mossy base of a tree, in a prairie fescue meadow, or along the trail in sunny open spots. This is a miniature study in beauty. Look carefully, and you will see that, like most violets, the flower has stripes. These stripes lead bees to the nectar and thereby ensure that the flower will be pollinated. Under infrared light, at a wavelength seen by bees, these stripes form an obvious guide – almost like an approach and landing strip for an airplane!

It is along this stretch of Quarry Road Trail that, in early June, you may hear a wonderful bird song from the dense cover of the shrubs and the Balsam Poplars. The song is loud and with a downward trill. The descending trill almost seems to have double notes and a touch of twang. It is, once again, the song of a Veery. This thrush is seldom seen but its unmistakable melody is a delight to hear! It feeds on the ground. Another species you may hear and see is the brilliant orange and black Baltimore Oriole.

Continuing down Quarry Road Trail, you will come to a minor washout on the left side of the road where planks have been installed to reduce erosion. About 50 metres beyond this point, as the path bends to the right, a great view of the Bow River opens up. In contrast to its single-channel nature under the Boothman Foot Bridge, the Bow is a multi-channel river at this point, flowing around unvegetated gravel bars and vegetated islands. The gravel bars are inundated every year during spring runoff, and lower vegetated islands may be partly submerged. The higher islands generally stay dry even during the runoff season. During large floods, however, like those that occurred around the beginning of the 20th Century, such islands would not only be submerged, but possibly also eroded away in part or whole. The Bow River here undoubtedly will have a different arrangement of bars and islands after the next big flood. Gravel that is removed here during a flood will be redeposited on a bar or island elsewhere downstream: it is the fate of river bedload to move down the river in fits and starts, with long rest periods in between.

Upstream and across the river, below the four red towers of McMahon Stadium, a sharp demarcation is seen between (1) the level bench underlying the university campus and University Heights community, and (2) the low ground along the river (part of the community of Montgomery). The steep wall between the two is a product of downcutting of the Bow River through the glacial deposits and lake sediments comprising the upper bench.

On mid-summer days, you might see the large American White Pelicans on the Bow River. These pelicans have been seen in an area of the Bow just east of Lawrey Gardens, an area with gravel bars and a low island. It is at such a site where you might expect to see pelicans fishing.[12] American White Pelicans, formerly an endangered species in Alberta,

TOP *American White Pelican* © Anthony Heazell

MIDDLE *Yellow Warbler (male)* © Wayne Lynch

BOTTOM *Song Sparrow* © Wayne Lynch

favour "shallow turbid lake…[habitat] with extensive shallows near shore and good rough fish populations".[13] They usually nest on low, flat treeless islands away from humans and predators.[14]

Although usually seen further downstream at Inglewood Bird Sanctuary and further south and east, pelicans may be beginning to populate the western stretches of the Bow. The Pelicans seen near Lawrey Gardens were probably juveniles. Whether they will form a colony in this area remains to be seen.

As the path continues eastward, you will see to your right the trestle bridge on Shaganappi Golf Course. This area was used for downhill skiing many years ago. Quarry Road Trail ends shortly thereafter, where it T's against a paved trail. The paved trail heading south climbs uphill along the edge of the golf course. Our route goes north (left) across the railway tracks to the paved regional pathway along the Bow River, where we turn left (west). This regional pathway is a busy area for cyclists, many of them in a hurry. Caution should be exercised.

As you continue west, the view of the Bow River becomes obscured by increasingly dense shrubbery, mostly introduced Caragana and some willows.

Here, you are likely to hear or see a Yellow Warbler. If you only catch a glimpse of it from afar, you may wonder "who let the canary out of its cage?". Although "misidentified as a 'wild canary' by some"[15], it is easy to recognize. A closer view will show the male's "brilliant yellow with olive-green wings and reddish breast streaks".[16] It is often difficult to see the Yellow Warbler because it blends into the yellowish-green leaves of Aspen trees or Sandbar Willows. Its song, "Sweet, sweet, sweet so sweet", is unmistakable as it searches for insects such as "caterpillars … and aphids".[17]

We are now approaching Lawrey Gardens to our right (north). You will notice three upright white/red barriers or bollards to your right (north). Turn onto this pathway and continue down the small hill. You have arrived at Lawrey Gardens, once referred to as the "Crown Jewel of the Parks system".[18] The barriers have been placed here so that cyclists will avoid the sharp turn and continue onto the new regional pathway further to the west but there may still be cyclists on this older pathway so exercise caution.

Almost immediately, you are walking through mature Balsam Poplars. Many migratory warblers visit this area in spring and fall and some nest here in the summer. There are many surprises for the birder. Here, for example, early one spring, a Western Bluebird was seen. On a hot July day, as we walked on the regional pathway just before the turn at the barriers, we heard the strident call of a baby Baltimore Oriole demanding to be fed. High in a Balsam Poplar tree, we could just see the hanging nest woven from grasses. A few days later, we saw the parents feeding their young which had fledged. At the same time, from a thicket of bushes, we heard a Song Sparrow calling "Pres-Pres-Pres byterian!!" – a song which it may repeat as many as 6-8 times per minute.[19]

We had just turned the corner when we saw the white-tipped tail feathers of an Eastern Kingbird. Suddenly, a battle erupted between the kingbird and a crow as the kingbird protected its nest nearby and its territory.

To the right of the path (before the path turns left) is a park bench overlooking the little cove made by the Bow River. Have a rest on this park bench. You may see a beaver or perhaps a muskrat. Many of the larger Balsam Poplars have been wrapped with wire for protection against the sharp teeth of a dam-building beaver.

Here, you might watch the grace of a park-user fly-fishing for trout in the large eddy created by the cove. The Bow River, through the Edworthy area, is a treasure trove for the fly fisherman. Looking down to the River, you may see an occasional huge trout

ABOVE *Lawrey Gardens, Alison Jackson Collection* © Calgary Public Library

resting near a log under the water.

As you walk in this area in the spring, you may see Canada Geese with their yellow, fluffy goslings eating grass or weeds next to the bench. Do not approach too closely so that you do not upset the parents or you may suffer from a "goose attack".

During the migration season, a variety of shorebirds may be seen from this point of land. Here, when the river was open one December, a Trumpeter Swan floated in shallow waters. It is unusual to see a swan so late. Although swan sightings are rare in the Edworthy area, the chance exists that overhead you may see a flock flying north in spring or south in fall.

You never know what may be seen or heard in the park because it is a migratory corridor for birds. Sometimes, when bad weather surrounds the City, migrating birds which might otherwise bypass the park stopover until the storm front passes. Such may have been the case when a loud trumpeting sound was heard, somewhat resembling a loud, sick-sounding goose. We were treated to the sight of a Sandhill Crane, long neck extended, as it flew over the escarpment in late April. Four hours later, the weather changed from Chinook conditions to a late spring snowstorm.

In spring, you may find attractive butterflies here. Brush piles and leaf litter are home to overwintering adult butterflies, including

TOP *Cat-tails* © Paul Beaulieu
BOTTOM LEFT *Hedge Bindweed* © L. McConnell
BOTTOM RIGHT *Satyr Anglewing* © E. Gilliam

anglewings. As their name suggests, the edges of their wings are cut and sharply angled. In recent years, near this area, Satyr Anglewings have repeatedly been observed. Like the Mourning Cloak, the Satyr Anglewing, when its wings are folded, is a non-descript mottled brown – perfect camouflage to blend into the dried, dead leaves of early spring. Here, in mid-summer, White Admiral butterflies enjoy Balsam Poplar leaves sticky with resin.

Continue along the old regional pathway. Twenty-five metres beyond the bench a gravel path branches left, away from the

paved pathway, and crosses the alternative paved pathway for cyclists. Follow this gravel road and continue to the west, underneath some utility pole wires. As you walk, notice the riverine vegetation; here Balsam Poplars grow with an undergrowth of Red-osier Dogwoods beyond the Caraganas.

Lawrey Gardens has some very old Caragana hedges, some dating to the time when John Lawrey homesteaded on the land and afterwards when a number of squatters lived in houses in the area. Settlers planted Caragana, native to Siberia, around their homes. To this day, you still may envision where such houses were located because of rows of this shrub.

Again, in mid-summer, you will see a small patch of Common Yarrow. Throughout most of the park, this plant has clusters of small, white flowers. Here, however, you may notice that the yarrow is a delicate shade of pink.

On the opposite side of the path, to the north, you may notice what looks, from afar, like a pale pink rose. Upon careful inspection, you will notice a pink flower which looks like a morning glory and indeed is a member of the Morning Glory Family. This is *Convolvulus sepia* or Hedge Bindweed.

Just after the utility poles run out, a narrow gravelled path goes to the left, to a pond, situated a few metres to the south. It is aptly named Willow Pond. This depression appears to be part of an old, long-abandoned channel of the Bow River. The City re-contoured the edges of this pond to restore a natural shape to it and undertook an extensive weed elimination program in the flat areas to the north and west. Native vegetation was replanted. Balsam Poplars did not seem to be rejuvenating in the area, but after the program eliminated the introduced Brome Grass, tiny Balsam Poplar shoots began to grow within two years.

Willow Pond is thriving now. As part of the program, the pond edges were replanted with Wide-leaved Cat-tails, and, within two years, the cat-tails had re-colonized a significant portion of the pond. Although this plant reproduces in part by seeds, it also propagates by sending out creeping roots. "The main stalk branches through the mud and sends up new leafy stems every spring. Finally it decays and all the new stems become plants in their turn".[20]

In spring, when the water level is high, Willow Pond is very beautiful with its graceful old willows overhanging the water. The old logs left in the Pond provide valuable habitat for birds and frogs alike. Here a Killdeer was once seen walking back and forth, back and forth, countless times, along one of these dead logs. Mallards and American Wigeons regularly visit. The pond is partially spring-fed and partially fed by storm sewer water. It is therefore advisable not to wade in this pond.

On a walk in spring, you may see a Mourning Cloak butterfly winging its way over the water. You may also hear the shrill call of a male Red-winged Blackbird or see its brilliant red shoulder patches.

In late May or early June, after dusk when all else is still, the croaking of frogs may be heard all the way up to Cedar Crescent above the escarpment. Somewhat later, tadpoles may be seen in the shallow waters of the pond. By July, it is possible to see tiny frogs along the shore of the pond – frogs which have finished their metamorphosis from tadpoles.

At one time, there were three species of frogs in the park – Leopard, Wood and Chorus frogs. Leopard Frogs have not been seen recently and are considered extirpated. It has been speculated that they may be declining because of sensitivity to changed levels of ozone. In their book, *The Amphibians and Reptiles of Alberta*, Anthony Russell and Aaron Bauer suggest that disease as well as pesticides and herbicides and, perhaps, several drought years may have played a role in the decline of the Northern Leopard Frog.[21]

TOP *Northern Leopard Frog* © Wayne Lynch

MIDDLE *Wood Frog* © Wayne Lynch

BOTTOM *Boreal Chorus Frog* © Wayne Lynch

Described as being predominantly green-ish or brownish with dark spots encircled by pale rings[22], the Northern Leopard Frog hibernates underneath the mud. An individual may travel up to 2 kilometres during a single active season. It eats insects, spiders, small birds, garter snakes, tadpoles and smaller frogs. In turn, the tadpoles are eaten by salamanders and garter snakes; adult frogs by birds.[23]

A Wood Frog is easily identified. It is small to medium-sized with a pale cream-coloured stripe running from its nose through the centre of its back. The distinguishing mark is a chocolate-brown triangle that runs halfway through the frog's eye. The upper portion of the eye is a golden colour whereas the lower portion is chocolate brown. The rest of the triangle forms a bandit-like patch of chocolate brown. Unlike the Leopard Frog, it is still relatively plentiful. Russell and Bauer describe the Wood Frog as being:

...chiefly diurnal and is found in wooded areas or associated with open ponds. It occurs up to 2,500 m elevation and is very cold-tolerant and hibernates on land beneath litter and humus. This species employs physicochemical mechanisms to protect against extreme cold and dryness. It forages widely, often far from water, and eats molluscs, worms, insects and other arthropods. [24]

The other species of frog found in the park is the small Boreal Chorus Frog. According to Russell and Bauer, it

...frequents grassy pools, lakes, marshes and almost any other body of water. It occurs on farms and even in cities, where suitable habitat is present, except where pesticides are heavily used. It eats ground-dwelling insects, snails, millipedes and other small invertebrates. [25]

They describe its call as "a terminally inflected trill that sounds like that generated when one's finger is run along the teeth of a stiff plastic pocket comb".[26] On a May day, we heard the distinctive croaking of Boreal Chorus Frogs at Willow Pond.

The two species of frogs found in the park (and the Leopard Frog) hibernate over winter. It is important not to walk on the semi-frozen surfaces of the Ponds so that you do not disturb or destroy the frogs.

Please do not pick up frogs in the park as doing so stresses them. Moreover, Wood Frogs have a protective mucus which may sting the human skin.

The city by-law prohibiting collection of natural objects includes tadpoles and frogs.

In the case of Wood Frogs, every female removed from a pond deprives the pond of 2,000 to 3,000 eggs per year. Collection would rapidly destroy the frog population here. Please leave them alone so that everyone may enjoy them, as tadpoles and later as small frogs, and hear their croaks. Even taking one frog could damage the population in the park.

Leaving Willow Pond, continue westward on the gravel path. You are approaching the area where John Lawrey homesteaded in the 1880s. The log cabin he originally built was eventually replaced by a white frame house, long since destroyed.

By the time the railway arrived, Lawrey had established a thriving market garden in the fertile river bottom soil and regularly entered his produce in competition at the Annual Fall Fairs, forerunner of the Calgary Exhibition. His entries were frequent winners. His market gardens barely met the demands of the Police Post and the tiny settlement.[27]

In part, Lawrey's success in market gardening was due to the rich soil; also helpful was the proximity of water from the Bow River which he used to irrigate his crops.

Lawrey Gardens, through the years, had a varied and colourful history. It is a great pity that in 1973 some of the rubble from the demolition of the Robin Hood Flour Mills was deposited on one part of Lawrey Gardens. The portion mined for gravel in the early 1950s by Andy Baxter is the same area where rubble was dumped in 1973. Since the dumping, frost heave has thrust some of this concrete rubble out of the ground. More recently, the City of Calgary has undertaken a rehabilitation of this area, consolidating the rubble into one central area, and planting native grasses and shrubs.

Even to this day, however, there are pristine areas on Lawrey Gardens unrivalled for unusual and rare wildflowers and bird life – including songbirds and birds of prey.

Lawrey Gardens is known for its unusual and rare vegetation. The best way for the reader to see these plants is to contact the Calgary Field Naturalists' Society which offers guided botany walks here every year.

One of the loveliest plants so observed is the Franklin's Lady's-slipper Orchid. It is a pale cream colour with speckled purple spots on the bottom of the pouch. The pouch also resembles the speckled egg of the sparrow – hence its other common name of Sparrow's-Egg Lady's-slipper.[28] A misplaced footstep or an errant bicycle tire can easily destroy these orchids. If the flower is picked, it wilts and the plant dies.

Another orchid is the beautiful Round-leaved Orchid. Both orchids have very specific requirements to survive: moist, acid soils. The Round-leaved Orchid has a single round or oval-shaped leaf at the base of the plant. It has been described accurately as exquisite.[29] Its white flower has a lip speckled with magenta spots. Its seeds only germinate and survive if a specific fungus is present in the soil, a fungus that helps the plant absorb nutrients.[30]

Some other plants in this area are often found in the mountains but are unusual in Calgary. One is the Few-flowered or Small Wood Anemone which "prefers moist soils". It has basal leaves that are divided into three "leaflets". Each stalk supports a single white flower.[31] It is a delightful flower, rare in the Edworthy area, perhaps the only site in Calgary.

In the same general vicinity, is the intriguing plant, Elephanthead. Look closely at its spike of flowers and you will observe that each flower resembles the head and upturned trunk of an elephant. It grows in wet areas and is most numerous along the river shoreline.

Grass-of-Parnassus grows near streams. It has a clump of heart-shaped leaves. Its white blooms are quite showy. Its common

RIGHT *Elephanthead* © O.F. Wachtler

TOP *Franklin's Lady's-slipper Orchid* © O.F. Wachtler
BOTTOM *Round-leaved Orchid* © O.F. Wachtler

name derives from the mountain of Parnassus in Greece, although the reason behind the name is unclear. The plant has no resemblance to grass. At the base of each petal is a false stamen that attracts pollinating insects.[32] Although the species observed in the mountains is Fringed Grass-of-Parnassus, the species found in Edworthy Park is an unfringed species, Northern Grass-of-Parnassus.

In addition, in the area being described is a unique plant called the "Common Butterwort". At first glance, you might mistake its purple blossom for that of a violet. Closer inspection will quickly reveal that this is a butterwort. Look at its leaves with their rolled-in edges. Perhaps you will be lucky enough to see an insect captured in the sticky substance exuded by its leaves. After being captured, such insects are digested by enzymes. This plant, more commonly seen in the mountains, is one of the few carnivorous plants found in Alberta. Why is this plant carnivorous? It is

thought that the insects so digested by the plant provide nutrients such as phosphorous and nitrogen that are otherwise not available to the plant in its wet habitat.[33]

Nearby, you may also see shooting stars and Mealy Primroses. The shooting stars, primroses, Elephanthead, Few-flowered Anemones, butterworts, and the orchids – both Franklin's Lady's-slipper and Round-leaved – are in bloom at about the same time, late June to early July.

We return to the description of our route and leave you to discover the rare plants described above on a CFNS walk. For now, however, you soon leave the Balsam Poplars behind and pass through open grasslands. This is an area rich in butterflies. Here, on a July day, in the weedy grass beside the road, a Milbert's Tortoise Shell butterfly landed. In less than a second, it was chased off by a Painted Lady butterfly. Nearby, a small Tawny-edged

LEFT Common Butterwort © O.F. Wachtler

TOP Western Wood-Pewee © E. Gilliam

MIDDLE Milbert's Tortoise Shell butterfly © O.F. Wachtler

BOTTOM LEFT Insects captured on Common Butterwort leaves, being digested © Wayne Lynch

BOTTOM RIGHT Mealy Primrose © O.F. Wachtler

Skipper landed on purple Dame's Rocket, an introduced flowering plant.

Walk westward until the dirt road merges with the regional pathway. In mid-July, we reached this intersection and were captivated by the behaviour of a Western Wood-Pewee. This flycatcher perched high up on a dead branch of a Balsam Poplar tree. With its sharp eyes, it kept watch for insects. When the pewee saw an insect, it would fly from its perch, swoop and catch the insect in mid-air, then return to its perch. Time after time, the pewee repeated its mid-air performance. It was hunting to keep its voracious young well fed. The nest was nearby, on a horizontal branch, where, just before dusk, the last light of the day reflected off the downy heads of the young.

The area next to the regional pathway is a good place to see garter snakes sunning themselves on rocks. Reptiles regulate their body temperature by basking in the sun. What better place to warm up than on a heat-reflecting rock? The two species of garter snake found in Edworthy Park and in Lawrey Gardens are the Wandering Garter Snake and the Red-sided Garter Snake.[34]

Undoubtedly, garter snakes are attracted to this area by plentiful food sources, including, as mentioned before, the possibility of tadpoles and young frogs. These snakes are harmless. If, however, you pick one up, you will regret it as it exudes a foul-smelling material.

This area is a birder's paradise! The combination of several habitat types – the river and its shore, the riverine shrubs and other vegetation, pond, open field, and coniferous trees – creates an environment which attracts a wealth of bird life. Here, you will pass nesting boxes placed in the Balsam Poplar trees for Wood Ducks. Before the 1980s, it was uncommon to see these ducks in Calgary but a few were released in Inglewood from a breeding program at Brooks and subsequently the species became more common. Other ducks such

ABOVE *Red-sided Garter Snake* © Wayne Lynch

as Common Goldeneyes and Common Mergansers may nest in these boxes.

Continue along the regional pathway until you have safely crossed the marked level railway crossing. Just beyond and above you is the Wildwood Slide, described in Walk Four. A few metres from the chain-link gate is a gravel pathway leading to the east. Meanwhile, at the "Slide Area No Stopping" sign, the paved regional pathway is intersected by a wide gravel path climbing up to the west and a narrower path climbing to the south and marked with a trail sign. There are two picturesque ways to head eastward from this point back toward the Quarry Road Trail; one follows the gravel pathway along the chainlink fence leading to the east (the informally named South Sora Pond Trail) and the other follows the path up the staircase to the south and joins the eastbound Douglas Fir Trail.

TOP *Wood Duck* © Kathleen Roman

BOTTOM *American Wigeon Duck* © Wayne Lynch

TOP *Common Goldeneye (male)* © Kathleen Roman

BOTTOM *Common Merganser* © Kathleen Roman

ALTERNATIVE A:
THE SOUTH SORA POND TRAIL

This alternative route eastward, following the lowlands close to the CPR tracks, has much to recommend it, particularly the great variety of wildflowers next to the path, and a pond with its associated vegetation. The trail begins where the regional pathway crosses the tracks. Just a few metres south of the chain-link gate by the track crossing, our route is on a gravelled pathway leading to the east, parallel to the tracks.

The path is bordered by a wonderful combination of prairie, boreal and wetland flowers. In the spring there are crocuses, Cut-leaved Anemones and, later in the summer, Gaillardia and other typical prairie wildflowers. Here along the edges of the path is one of the few places in the park where Sticky False Asphodel grows. A small plant, Sticky False Asphodel has three or four iris-like leaves at the base. Its flower is a small white cluster with darker

anthers at the top.[35] Here prairie meets pond – for Sticky False Asphodel is a wildflower that grows near the edges of bogs and ponds. Even more rare is a Dwarf False Asphodel also found in this vicinity.

In this area grows a magnificent patch of Kinnikinnick or Common Bearberry. We described this plant in Walk Four but it is along this trail that it grows profusely and is readily observed. Here in spring you may see its leathery-green leaves hugging the ground or its tiny pink urn-shaped flowers. From mid-summer to fall, you may see its bright red berries.

After a couple hundred metres from the regional pathway, you will see (and may hear!) the other major frog pond in Edworthy Park, informally called the South Sora Pond. There is a sign requesting the public not to remove anything from the pond or to enter it. This is good advice, considering the soft mud and the rotten egg smell generated by the mud's disturbance (hydrogen sulphide produced by the anaerobic pond bottom).

It is advisable not to wade in the water for other reasons – a number of creosoted railway ties were resting in the pond for several years. Creosote is a known carcinogen and traces of creosote might remain in this pond. When the Douglas Fir Trail was rebuilt in the early 1990s, two large jet plane tires were removed by helicopter from the water. When the water level was low, this pond, its vegetation and animal life also suffered because of off-trail mountain biking through it. Fortunately, the level rose and this problem seems to have ended. It is important to keep dogs from wading in the pond and its vegetation because that has been proven to have a detrimental effect on pond wildlife and shore-nesting birds (and the dogs themselves).

The cat-tails in this pond have recovered, spread, and today form a healthy habitat. Amid the cat-tails and bulrushes, you may notice a dull brownish-black bird – at first glance, you may think it is a large sparrow but look again. This is a female Red-winged Blackbird. She has a "light streak over the crown and above the eye". We all know the male blackbird with its "red and buffy wing epaulets".[36] Here is its prime nesting habitat – location, location, location! Its nest is woven from grasses and situated in the vegetation near the water.

Also, in this vicinity, you may see an Eastern Kingbird again. This conspicuous black and white bird is easily identified. One distinguishing mark is the black tail feathers rimmed with a white bottom edge. Less frequently seen is its red or orange concealed crown – raised and therefore more clearly visible when the bird is attacking an intruder.[37] Tarry awhile and you may see the Eastern Kingbird swooping from its perch to catch insects near the pond. The kingbird is a flycatcher and like all flycatchers catches insects while on the wing.

The pond itself is the southern extension of the Sora Slough. Soras are a species of

LEFT *Alpine Bistort* © L. McConnell
RIGHT *Sticky False Asphodel* © L. McConnell

rail – an elusive bird you are more likely to hear than see. Its vocal "whinny" is unmistakable. It frequents pond edge vegetation of cat-tails, rushes or sedges for concealment. Soras feed on molluscs, mosquitoes and dragonflies.[38]

One July day at the edge of the Pond, the silence was broken by the striking call of the Sora. We then were treated to the sight of an adult Sora swimming in and out of the cat-tails from the far side towards the near shore, to lead a chick back across the pond to safety.

On this same day, we also saw some lovely white flowers floating on the water. They were a member of the Buttercup Family called "White Water Buttercup or Crowfoot". White Water Crowfoot is buoyed up and given structure by air pockets in its underwater stems. If this plant is removed from the water, it collapses into a formless mass.[39]

At all of the ponds and sloughs in the area, vegetation abounds. Here you may see an abundance of sedges and rushes. To distinguish them, there is a saying – "sedges have edges, rushes are round." Keep this in mind as you look closely at the stalk of a plant to help identify it.

Near the edge of the Pond, horsetail-like plants grow out of the water. These Mare's-tails differ from horsetail or *Equisetum* by

being a flowering plant, unlike *Equisetum* which is spore-bearing. Near the path are shrubby Water Birches, with dark bark unlike the white bark of the European Weeping Birches that grow in city yards. The many seed heads support a variety of bird species and are a favourite food of the Golden-crowned Kinglet.

Arrowhead with its distinctly-shaped leaf grows near the water's edge. This was an important food source for the native people as they harvested the underwater bulbs. Cat-tails were also an important source of food and the pollen provided flour. Cat-tails also were woven to make mats.

At South Sora Pond, as at Willow Pond, you may see tadpoles of Wood Frogs, Boreal Chorus Frogs and perhaps, even, the now rare Leopard Frog. Here also you might see a nocturnal Tiger Salamander. In early spring, adult salamanders migrate to ponds to mate. From the time in early spring when eggs are laid, it takes three weeks to hatch into larva. According to Russell and Bauer, the larvae take three to four months and sometimes as long as two years to metamorphose into salamanders.[40]

Since salamanders "lay their eggs attached to stones, plants and debris", it is important not to wade in or otherwise disturb the pond and its vegetation. Adult salamanders feed on "insects, mites, earthworms, molluscs," etc. Hatchlings eat "zooplanktons" while older larvae and newly metamorphosed salamander (called neotenes) may eat "insect larvae and eggs, fish, frogs, and other salamanders," etc.[41]

The pond provides not only nesting habitat for birds and amphibians but also is a fabulous habitat for insects on which birds and amphibians rely. John Acorn coined the term, 'bugsters', for people who are interested in insects. It is at this pond that you might develop (or should we say "metamorphose"?) into a bugster.[42]

Here you may see damselflies and dragon-flies. Damselflies are slender and, at rest,

ABOVE *White Water Crowfoot* © Paul Beaulieu

they align their wings along their bodies and "all of their wings are similar in shape"; by contrast, dragonflies are larger, with wings permanently at right angles to their bodies and with "hindwings [which] are broader than forewings".[43] Both are ancient life forms, and date back to approximately 300 million years ago. It is intriguing to watch dragonflies as they fly over the pond to catch mosquitoes, their favourite food. Damselflies, being smaller, eat aphids and baby grasshoppers.[44] Some species of dragonflies stay near the pond of their hatching while others wander afar and may be seen in your garden.[45] Almost all of the species of damselflies – such as Boreal and Taiga Bluets – and of dragonflies – such as the Darners, Meadowhawks, Skimmers and Snaketails – may be observed at this pond and in Edworthy Park.

The top of the water sometimes seems alive! Small insects seem to drop down to skim and hop all over the surface of the water. Certainly at this pond you may see an aquatic insect called a water-strider or "Kayak Pond Skater", which can rest on and skim over the surface. How does it do this?

ABOVE *Tiger Salamander* © Wayne Lynch

Its weight is distributed over four extraordinarily long legs and its legs "repel water". This along with the surface tension of the water keeps the skater on top.[46]

You might wish to take a sketch pad with you to the pond. Take notes of what you see, drawing and labelling what you observe. Take a folding stool, place it where it will not damage the vegetation, and wait to see what appears. On one trip, we were rewarded by a duck with ten ducklings. On another trip, we saw an Eastern Kingbird. Insect repellent is useful if there are

TOP *Kayak Pond Skater (Water Strider)* © Paul Beaulieu
UPPER MIDDLE *Damselfly* © Wayne Lynch
LOWER MIDDLE *Adult Dragonfly emerging...* © Wayne Lynch
BOTTOM LEFT *Eyebright* © E. Gilliam
BOTTOM RIGHT *Seneca Snakeroot* © L. McConnell

mosquitoes that the dragonflies have not yet captured!

When ready to leave the pond, return to the gravel path. Although the path is marked as a no-bicycling zone, beware of errant high-speed cyclists.

Continuing eastward, you will find a wonderful grove of Wolf Willows in addition to the wildflowers that grow in the edge conditions of prairie, pond, and boreal and mixed woodland forests. In early June, you may be almost overpowered by the fragrance from its small yellow flowers.

In July, you may see three less commonly encountered plant species. A small patch of Eyebright on the south side of the path is a treat. Eyebright, as the name suggests, was used as an eyewash by settlers to treat eye problems.[47] It is rarely found outside of the foothills and mountains. This is one of only two locations known where it grows in Calgary.[48]

On either side of the path, you may discover Seneca Snakeroot. The plant has several spikes of closely packed flowers. The common name derives from the Seneca Indians, who lived in northeastern Oklahoma and the bordering areas of Arkansas and Missouri, and "who used the root as a treatment for snakebite (because the root resembles a snake)".[49] Another medicinal use was as an expectorant.[50] Like willows and aspens, it is a source of salicylic acid and methylsalicylate. Like buffaloberries, it contains saponins. Next to its qualities as a snakebite remedy, its best known use is to flavour candies and drinks.[51] Its presence along the edge of this path is not surprising as its usual habitat is along "edges of aspen groves, scrubby patches, and moist grassy meadows of the parklands"[52].

Nearby, you may also see Pale Comandra, a member of the Sandalwood Family. Its flowers in May or June vary in colour from greenish-white to pink and are "borne in clusters of three to five at the tips of stems". This plant prefers dry conditions. The variation in

moisture along this path in part accounts for the diversity of plant species and contributes to the unique nature of the area.[53]

Near a shiny metal equipment box next to the railway, you may encounter Pale Blue-eyed Grass, once again at the edges of the path. Although it is similar to Common Blue-eyed Grass described in Walk One, which also grows here, this species is a much paler shade of blue. This is a rare species seldom found in Alberta.

Slightly farther along, Saskatoons and other shrubs border the path. Here one early morning after a rainstorm, several species of butterflies, including fritillaries, landed on the path in front of us, and were "puddling". This term is used to describe the behaviour of butterflies when they alight on moist soil or mud to obtain moisture and minerals.

Soon you come to the intersection of this path with the Douglas Fir Trail (Alternative B) in the grassy meadow on the river terrace. The intersection is marked by a city map-sign and a no-bicycles sign. Continue eastward (left) on the Douglas Fir Trail to return to the Cedar Crescent parking lot, as described under Alternative B.

ALTERNATIVE B: DOUGLAS FIR TRAIL EAST

From the railway crossing, climb up the steps on the trail to the south, past the trail-map sign, to connect with the Douglas Fir Trail, where you will turn left (east). In mid-summer you may notice the white Canada Anemones blooming next to the steps.

As you head eastward, you will pass through coniferous woods. Here, as elsewhere on the trail, you may see a Red Squirrel. This is an indigenous species, unlike the black or grey-coloured squirrels often seen in yards and gardens. The latter are an imported species from Eastern Canada; a breeding pair was released from the Calgary Zoo in the Elbow Park district in the early 1940s and proceeded to colonize the City.[54] This

RIGHT Common Fireweed © Wayne Lynch

has been an unintended ecological disaster for the bird population of the City as these squirrels plunder birds' nests. Although you may occasionally see a Gray Squirrel along the Douglas Fir Trail, they are not common here. Probably they are captured by hawks and other predators in the forest. They are most readily seen in the picnic area.

Despite its smaller size, the Red Squirrel is feisty and can often be seen chasing the larger Gray Squirrels. On the Douglas Fir Trail, you may see a Red Squirrel eating the seeds from Douglas-fir or White Spruce cones. The pile of leftover scales is called a midden.

There are more bridges along this eastern portion of the Douglas Fir Trail. Standing on 5122F, one can see a scarp a few metres high, roughly 30 m uphill from the bridge. This is probably the headwall of an old slump. The general slope instability in the area between bridges F and G is indicated by the many "drunken" trees.

Between bridges F and G, there are many rounded cobbles in and adjacent to the trail, especially on a small, flat bench traversed by the trail. Many of these have the little chip marks suggestive of travel in the bed of a river. Some of these cobbles probably have rolled down from above, but some may be *in-situ* on the bench, meaning that they might have been deposited right there by the Bow River, when the river bottom was at that level.

Bridge 5122G passes over another perennial spring-fed stream. East of the bridge, the trail leaves the forest and enters a meadow. This is probably an old river terrace, created by the Bow when it was getting close to its modern elevation. In this meadow, vast patches of Common Fireweed grow. In June, the meadow is also tinted purple with Dame's Rocket, an escaped cultivated plant belonging to the Mustard Family. You may also observe patches of vegetation which appear to have been compacted. These are deer beds – deer have rested here.

TOP *Canada Anemone* © O.F. Wachtler

MIDDLE *Red Squirrel* © E. Jones

BOTTOM *Rounded river gravel on a small bench on the Douglas Fir Trail* © J. Osborn

ABOVE *Mule Deer* © Wayne Lynch

Overhead, either above this meadow or closer to the pond, you may see an American Kestrel. It is the smallest raptor in North America. It prefers open areas and preys on "mice, voles, and insects – primarily grasshoppers". It also "occasionally hunts "birds, small reptiles and amphibians". The area of the meadow is ideal for the kestrel. On several occasions, we have observed a kestrel, in this area, hovering in the air "with its tail spread and wings beating rapidly".[55]

The Douglas Fir Trail meets the South Sora Pond Trail and then drops several metres to a lower bench, adjacent to the tracks. This bench is probably another, younger river terrace. The linear depression at the base of the escarpment is likely a fossil river channel.

After traversing the lowlands for a time, the trail abruptly turns right, toward the escarpment, and begins to climb through large White Spruce and Douglas-firs. Here, in

spring, as along more westerly portions of the Douglas Fir Trail, you may see a profusion of Western Canada White Violets and other wildflowers common to the boreal and montane areas of the trail.

As you climb the hillside, you leave the forest behind and pass through another edge condition, leading into a wonderful area of junipers and then prairie fescue grasslands. Here on the sunny slope, Prairie Crocuses grow in the middle of juniper patches. As you leave the junipers behind, more crocuses blooming in April announce the arrival of early spring in the fescue grassland.

This is where you may see a Coyote in search of mice or voles which live in the grassland. It is an on-leash area for dogs, in part due to some attacks by coyotes on dogs. Coyotes usually depart when they see a human, but, in this area, some Coyotes have become habituated to

people. Small dogs and roaming cats may be too much of a temptation for a hungry Coyote. Coyotes are magnificent animals. In addition to feeding on small mammals such as mice and rabbits, the Coyotes also eat low hanging berries such as Saskatoons and rose hips. In fact, up to 90% of their diet may be vegetation. Sometimes, in this area, especially in the mating season in early January and February, you may hear the yodelling of Coyotes. Occasionally, when a siren wails in the distance, the Coyotes join in – perhaps calling to their large metal counterparts.

From springtime onward, as dusk falls, you may be treated to the sight of Little Brown Bats flying through the air. This is mosquito control at its finest. It is intriguing to watch the bats swoop for insects overhead. If you see a bat at rest, leave it alone as bats can (though rarely do) carry rabies.

After a near-horizontal traverse the Douglas Fir Trail bends right (southward) and climbs the upper part of the escarpment. It connects back to the Quarry Road Trail a little over 100 m from the parking lot off Cedar Crescent. It is time to call it a day – or if you've been bat-watching, an evening!

TOP American Kestrel © Wayne Lynch
BOTTOM Coyote Pup © Wayne Lynch

ABOVE *Coyote Hunting* © *Wayne Lynch*

Footnotes – Walk Five

[1] As described in a letter from Bill Hilton to Ron Linden, quoted with permission from Ron Linden.

[2] Unattributed manuscript M6286, *William John Tregillus 1858-1914*, Glenbow Archives, p. 1.

[3] Annora Brown, *Old Man's Garden*, p. 24.

[4] *Ibid.* p. 23.

[5] *Ibid.* p. 99.

[6] George Scotter and Hälle Flygare, *Wildflowers of the Canadian Rockies*, p. 126.

[7] *The Calgary Tribune*, Wednesday Oct. 14, 1885.

[8] *The Regina Leader Post*, August 13, 1885. C.P.C. is a typographical error which presumably should read C.P.R.

[9] Federation of Alberta Naturalists, *The Atlas of Breeding Birds of Alberta*, p. 275.

[10] *Ibid.* p. 148.

[11] Annora Brown, *Op. Cit.*, p. 222.

[12] Federation of Alberta Naturalists, *The Atlas of Breeding Birds of Alberta*, p. 44.

[13] *Ibid.*

[14] *Ibid.*

[15] *Ibid.* p. 249.

[16] *Ibid.*

[17] *Ibid.*

[18] Thomas Mawson, *City of Calgary Past, Present & Future*, p. 48.

[19] Federation of Alberta Naturalists, *Op. Cit.*, p.289.

[20] Annora Brown, *Op. Cit.*, p. 80.

[21] Anthony P. Russell and Aaron M. Bauer, *The Amphibians and Reptiles of Alberta*, p. 83.

[22] *Ibid.* p. 80.

[23] *Ibid.* p. 82.

[24] *Ibid.* pp.84-86.

[25] *Ibid.* pp. 73-75.

[26] Anthony P. Russell and Aaron M. Bauer, *Op. Cit.*, p. 75.

[27] Edworthy Park Heritage Society, *Early Days in Edworthy Park and the Neighboring Areas of Brickburn and Lawrey Gardens*, p.26.

[28] George W. Scotter and Halle Flygare, *Wildflowers of the Canadian Rockies*, p. 40.

[29] *Ibid.*

[30] C. Dana Bush, *Op. Cit.*, p. 91.

[31] Scotter and Flygare, *Op. Cit.*, p. 54.

[32] Annora Brown, *Op. Cit.*, p. 145

[33] Scotter and Flygare, *Op. Cit.*, p. 148; and C.Dana Bush, *The Compact Guide to Wildflowers of the Rockies*, p. 91.

[34] Russell and Bauer, *Op. Cit.*, pp. 104-113.

[35] Scotter and Flygare, *Op. Cit.*, p. 34.

[36] Federation of Alberta Naturalists, *Op. Cit.*, p. 299.

[37] *Ibid.* p. 191.

[38] *Ibid.* p. 108.

[39] R.G.H. Cormack, *Wild Flowers of Alberta*, p. 111.

[40] Russell and Bauer, *Op. Cit.*, p. 56.

[41] *Ibid.*

[42] John Acorn, *Bugs of Alberta*, p.11.

[43] *Ibid.* p. 111.

[44] *Ibid.* p. 109.

[45] *Ibid.* p. 117.

[46] *Ibid.* p. 120.

[47] William A.R. Thomson M.D., editor, *Medicines from the Earth*, p. 89.

[48] The other location is at Paskapoo Slopes near 77th Street S.W.

[49] William A.R. Thomson, M.D., *Op. Cit.*, p. 181.

[50] *Ibid.*

[51] F.R. Vance, J.R. Jowsey, J.S. McLean and F.A. Switzer, *Wildflowers Across the Prairies*, p. 161.

[52] *Ibid.*

[53] *Ibid.* p. 58.

[54] Grant MacEwan, "Adventurous boy squirrel came home as a mom", *Calgary Herald*, Sat. Oct. 15, 1988

[55] Federation of Alberta Naturalists, *Op. Cit.*, p. 90.

© Marie Maitland

APPENDIX ONE

CHECKLIST OF VASCULAR PLANTS OF EDWORTHY PARK AND VICINITY

By Gustave J. Yaki, 2002

Below are the vascular plants recorded for the park and surrounding area. Non-native species are indicated by the plus (+) symbol. Those with an asterisk (*) were noted during four visits between 25 June-14 Sept. 2001. Species not in the "Calgary Natural Areas" Report on the Plants of Edworthy Park, published by the Calgary Field Naturalists' Society in 1980, are indicated by the chevron (^) symbol. Species are listed in taxonomic order. Within families they are arranged alphabetically by scientific name. For the most part they follow the names used in *Flora of Alberta*, by Moss, 1983. Space is provided to check off those you have identified. Should you be fortunate enough to find a new species, note its exact location, and notify the Edworthy Park Heritage Society and/or the Calgary Field Naturalists' Society, c/o <gyaki@calcna.ab.ca>.

SPORE-PRODUCING PLANTS - PTERIDOPHYTA

SPIKEMOSS FAMILY, SELAGINACEAE
☐ Little Spikemoss, *Selaginella densa*

HORSETAIL FAMILY, EQUISETACEAE
☐ Field Horsetail*, *Equisetum arvense*
☐ Swamp Horsetail* ^ , *E. fluviatile*
☐ Scouring Rush, *E. hyemale*
☐ Smooth Scouring Rush, *E. laevigatum*
☐ Meadow Horsetail* ^ , *E. pratense*
☐ Variegated Horsetail*, *E. variegatum*

FERN FAMILY, POLYPODIACEAE
☐ Fragile Fern, *Cystopteris fragilis*

SEED PRODUCING PLANTS - SPERMATOPHYTA

Seeds usually in dry cone - GYMNOSPERMAE

JUNIPER FAMILY, CUPRESSACEAE
☐ Common Juniper*, *Juniperus communis*
☐ Creeping Juniper*, *J. horizontalis*

PINE FAMILY, PINACEAE
☐ Japanese Larch+* ^ , *Larix japonica*
☐ White Spruce*, *Picea glauca*
☐ Blue Spruce+* ^ , *P. pungens*
☐ Douglas-fir*, *Pseudotsuga menziesii*

Seeds enclosed in an ovary - ANGIOSPERMAE

Seedlings with one leaf - MONOCOTYLEDONAE

CAT-TAIL FAMILY, TYPHACEAE
☐ Wide-leaved Cat-tail*, *Typha latifolia*

PONDWEED FAMILY, POTAMOGETONACEAE
☐ Pondweed sp.* ^ , *Potomogeton sp.* - in South Sora Pond.
☐ Sago Pondweed* ^ , *P. pectinatus*. In river.

ARROWGRASS FAMILY, JUNCAGINACEAE
☐ Slender Arrowgrass* ^ , *Triglochin palustris*

WATER-PLANTAIN FAMILY, ALISMATACEAE
☐ Arrowhead* ^ , *Sagittaria cuneata*

GRASS FAMILY, GRAMINEAE
☐ Crested Wheatgrass+*, *Agropyron pectiniforme*
☐ Quack Grass+*, *A. repens*
☐ Slender Wheatgrass, *A. trachycaulum*
☐ Redtop+, *Agrostis stolonifera*
☐ Wild Oat+*, *Avena fatua*,
☐ Cultivated Oat+*, *A. sativa*
☐ Slough Grass*, *Beckmannia syzigachne*
☐ Blue Grama Grass, *Bouteloua gracilis*
☐ Smooth Brome Grass+*, *Bromus inermis*
☐ Japanese Chess+, *B. japonicus*
☐ Downy Chess+* ^ , *B. tectorum*
☐ Marsh Reed Grass, *Calamagrostis canadensis*
☐ Northern Reed Grass, *C. inexpansa*
☐ Sand Grass, *Calamovilfa longifolia*
☐ Brook Grass, *Catabrosa aquatica*
☐ Orchard Grass+* ^ , *Dactylis glomerata*
☐ Parry's Oat Grass+* ^ , *Danthonia parryi*
☐ Canada Wild Rye, *Elymus canadensis*
☐ Hairy Wild Rye, *E. innovatus*
☐ Russian Wild Rye+*, *E. junceus*
☐ Giant Wild Rye, *E. piperi*
☐ Rough Fescue*, *Festuca scabrella*
☐ Fowl Manna Grass, *Glyceria striata*
☐ Hooker's Oat Grass, *Helictotricon hookeri*
☐ Sweet Grass*, *Hierochloe odorata*
☐ Foxtail Barley*, *Hordeum jubatum*
☐ Cultivated Barley+*, *H. vulgare*
☐ June Grass*, *Koelaria macrantha*
☐ Perennial Rye Grass+, *Lolium perenne*
☐ Cut-leaved Ricegrass* ^ , *Oryzopsis asperifolia*
☐ Switch Grass+* ^ , *Panicum virgatum*
☐ Timothy+*, *Phleum pratense*
☐ Annual Bluegrass+, *Poa annua*
☐ Canada Bluegrass+, *P. compressa*
☐ Skyline Bluegrass, *P. epilis*
☐ Fowl Bluegrass, *P. palustris*
☐ Kentucky Bluegrass+, *P. pratensis*
☐ Cultivated Rye+, *Secale cereale*
☐ Green Foxtail+, *Setaria viridis*
☐ Spear Grass, *Stipa comata*
☐ Green Needle Grass*, *Stipa viridula*
☐ Cultivated Wheat+*, *Triticum aestivum*

SEDGE FAMILY, CYPERACEAE
☐ Water Sedge, *Carex aquatilis*
☐ Golden Sedge*, *C. aurea*
☐ Hair-like Sedge, *C. capillaris*
☐ Beaked Sedge, *C. rostrata*

☐ Sprengel's Sedge, *C. sprengelii*
☐ Needle Spikerush, *Eleocharis acicularis*
☐ Creeping Spikerush, *E. palustris*
☐ Great Bulrush*^, *Scirpus validus*

RUSH FAMILY, JUNCACEAE

☐ Alpine Rush, *Juncus alpinoarticulatus*
☐ Wire Rush*, *J. balticus*
☐ Knotted Rush, *J. nodosus*

LILY FAMILY, LILIACEAE

☐ Nodding Onion*, *Allium cernuum*
☐ Wild Chives*, *A. schoenprasum*
☐ Prairie Onion*, *A. textile*
☐ Garden Asparagus+*^, *Asparagus officinalis*
☐ Lily-of-the-Valley+*^, *Convallaria majalis*
☐ Rough-fruited Fairy-bells*, *Disporum tachycarpum*
☐ Western Wood Lily*, *Lilium philadelphicum*
☐ False Solomon's-seal*, *Smilacina racemosa*
☐ Star-flowered Solomon's-seal*, *S. stellata*
☐ Twisted-stalk, *Streptopus amplexifolius*
☐ Sticky False Asphodel*, *Tofieldia glutinosa*
☐ Dwarf False Asphodel*^, *T. pusilla*
☐ White Camas*, *Zigadenus elegans*
☐ Death Camas, *Z. venenosis*

IRIS FAMILY, IRIDACEAE

☐ Bearded Iris+, *Iris missourensis*
☐ Common Blue-eyed Grass*, *Sisyrinchium montanum*
☐ Pale Blue-eyed Grass*, *S. septentrionale*

ORCHID FAMILY, ORCHIDACEAE

☐ Spotted Coralroot^, *Corallorhiza maculata*
☐ Striped Coralroot, *C.striata*
☐ Early Coralroot*, *C. trifida*
☐ Yellow Lady's-slipper, *Cypripedium calceolus*
☐ Sparrow's-egg Lady's-slipper*, *C. passerinum*
☐ Northern Green Orchid*, *Platanthera hyperborea*
☐ Bracted Green Orchid, *P. viridis*
☐ Round-leaved Orchis*, *Orchis rotundifolia*

Seedlings with two leaves - DICOTYLEDONAE

WILLOW FAMILY, SALICACEAE

☐ Balsam Poplar*, *Populus balsamifera*
☐ Swedish Columnar Poplar+*^, *P. tremula Erecta*
☐ Trembling Aspen*, *P. tremuloides*
☐ NorthWest Poplar+*^, *P. x jackii Northwest*
☐ Peach-leaf Willow, *Salix amygdaloides*
☐ Beaked Willow*, *S. bebbiana*
☐ Short-capsuled Willow, *S. brachycarpa*
☐ Hoary Willow, *S. candida*
☐ Pussy Willow, *S. discolor*
☐ Sandbar Willow*, *S. exigua*
☐ Yellow Willow, *S. lutea*

☐ Myrtle-leaved Willow, *S. myrtillifolia*
☐ Laurel-leaved Willow+*^, *S. pentandra*
☐ Plane-leaf Willow, *S. planifolia.*

BIRCH FAMILY, BETULACEAE

☐ River Alder, *Alnus tenufolia*
☐ Water Birch*, *Betula occidentalis*
☐ Paper Birch+*^, *B. papyrifera*
☐ Swamp Birch, *B. pumila*

BEECH FAMILY, FAGACEAE

☐ Bur Oak+*^, *Quercus macrocarpa*

ELM FAMILY, ULMACEAE

☐ American Elm+*^, *Ulmus americana*

HEMP FAMILY, CANNABINACEAE

☐ Common Hop+, *Humulus lupulus*

NETTLE FAMILY, URTICACEAE

☐ Stinging Nettle*, *Urtica dioica*

SANDALWOOD FAMILY, SANTALACEAE

☐ Bastard Toad-flax*, *Comandra umbellata*

BUCKWHEAT FAMILY, POLYGONACEAE

☐ Yellow Umbrella-plant*, *Eriogonum flavum*
☐ Common Buckwheat+*, *Fagopyron esculentum*
☐ Tartary Buckwheat+ *F. tartaricum*
☐ Common Knotweed+*, *Polygonum arenastrum*
☐ Striate Knotweed, *P. erectum*
☐ Wild Buckwheat+, *P. convolvulus*
☐ Alpine Bistort*, *P. viviparum*
☐ Curled Dock+*^, *Rumex crispus*
☐ Golden Dock, *R. maritimus*
☐ Western Dock, *R. occidentalis*
☐ Narrow-leaved Dock*, *R. trangulivalvis*

GOOSEFOOT FAMILY, CHENIPODIACEAE

☐ Garden Orache+, *Atriplex hortensis*
☐ Prostrate Saltbush+, *A. prostrata*
☐ Russian Pigweed+, *Axyris amaranthoides*
☐ Lambs Quarters+*, *Chenopodium album*
☐ Maple-leafed Goosefoot, *C. gigantospermum*
☐ Summer-cypress+*^, *Kochia scoparia*

AMARANTH FAMILY, AMARANTHACEAE

☐ Red-root Pigweed +, *Amaranthus retroflexus*

PINK FAMILY, CAROPHYLLACEAE

☐ Field Chickweed, *Cerastium arvense*
☐ Baby's Breath+*^, *Gypsophilla paniculata*
☐ Blunt-leaved Sandwort*, *Moehringia lateriflora*
☐ Soapwort+*^, *Saponaria officinalis*
☐ Smooth Catchfly+, *Silene cserei*
☐ Bladder Campion+*^, *S. cucubalus*
☐ White Cockle+*, *S. pratensis*
☐ Long-stalked Chickweed, *Stellaria longipes*
☐ Common Chickweed+, *S. media*

☐ Cow-cockle+, *Vaccaria pyramidata*

CROWFOOT FAMILY, RANUNCULACEAE
☐ Red Baneberry*, *Actaea rubra*
☐ Canada Anemone*, *Anemone canadensis*
☐ Long-fruited Anemone*, *A. cylindrica*
☐ Cut-leaved Anemone*, *A. multifida*
☐ Small Wood Anemone* ^, *A. parviflora*
☐ Prairie Crocus*, *A. patens*
☐ Blue Columbine*, *Aquilegia brevistyla*
☐ Western Clematis, *Clematis ligusticifolia*
☐ Purple Clematis*, *C. occidentalis*
☐ Yellow Clematis+*, *C. tangutica*
☐ Tall Larkspur*, *Delphinium glaucum*
☐ Garden Larkspur+*^, *D. sp. (Pale blue)*
☐ Small-flowered Buttercup*, *Ranunculus abortivus*
☐ Tall Buttercup+*, *R. acris*
☐ White Water Buttercup*^, *R. circinatus*
☐ Seaside Buttercup*, *R. cymbalaria*
☐ Early Buttercup, *R. glaberrinus*
☐ Macoun's Buttercup*, *R. macounii*
☐ Creeping Spearwort*^, *R. reptans*
☐ Tall Meadow Rue*^, *Thalictrum dasycarpum*
☐ Veiny Meadow Rue*, *T. venulosum*

FUMITORY FAMILY, FUMIARACEAE
☐ Golden Corydalis*, *Corydalis aurea*

MUSTARD FAMILY, CRUCIFERAE
☐ Hirsute Rock Cress, *Arabis hirsuta*
☐ Reflexed Rock Cress, *A. holboellil*
☐ Horseradish+*^, *Armoracia rusticana*
☐ Rape/Canola+*, *Brassica campestris*
☐ Indian Mustard+, *B. juncea*
☐ Charlock+, *B. kaber*
☐ Shepherd's-purse+, *Capsella bursa-pastoris*
☐ Grey Tansy Mustard, *Descuriania richardsonii*
☐ Flixweed+*, *D. sophia*
☐ Hoary Whitlow-grass, *Draba cana*
☐ Dog Mustard+, *Erucastrum gallicum*
☐ Wormseed Mustard, *Erysimum cheiranthoides*
☐ Small-flowered Rocket*, *E. inconspicuum*
☐ Dame's Rocket+*, *Hesperis matronalis*
☐ Common Peppergrass*, *Lepidium densiflorum*
☐ Branched Peppergrass*, *L. ramosissimum*
☐ Bladderpod, *Lesquerella arenosa*
☐ Marsh Yellow Cress*^, *Rorippa palustris*
☐ Tumbling Mustard+, *Sisymbrium altissimum*
☐ Tall Hedge Mustard+*, *S. loeselii*
☐ Stinkweed+*, *Thlaspi arvense*

SAXIFRAGE FAMILY, SAXIFRAGACEAE
☐ Alum-root*, *Heuchera richardsonii*

GRASS-OF-PARNASSUS FAMILY, PARNASSIACEAE
☐ Northern Grass-of-Parnassus*, *Parnassia palustris*

GOOSEBERRY FAMILY, GROSSULARIACEAE
☐ Currant sp.*, *Ribes sp.* 1 clump below west bridge on Douglas Fir Trail.
☐ Northern Gooseberry*, *Ribes oxyacanthoides*

ROSE FAMILY, ROSACEAE
☐ Saskatoon*, *Amelanchier alnifolia*
☐ Chamaerhodos, *Chamaerhodos erecta*
☐ Cotoneaster+*, *Cotoneaster acutifolia*
☐ Round-leaved Hawthorn* ^, *Crataegus rotundifolia*
☐ Wild Strawberry*, *Fragaria virginiana*
☐ Yellow Avens*, *Geum allepicum*
☐ Large-leaved Yellow Avens* ^, *G. macrophyllum*
☐ Three-flowered Avens*, *G. triflorum*
☐ Crabapple+*^, *Malus sp.*
☐ Silverweed*, *Potentilla anserina*
☐ White Cinquefoil*, *P. arguta*
☐ Early Cinquefoil, *P. concinna*
☐ Shrubby Cinquefoil*, *P. fruticosa*
☐ Woolly Cinquefoil, *P. hippiana*
☐ Rough Cinquefoil*, *P. norvegica*
☐ Prairie Cinquefoil, *P. pensylvanica*
☐ Mayday+*^, *Prunus padus*
☐ Common Chokecherry*, *P. virginiana*
☐ Ussurian Pear+*^, *Pyrus ussuriensis*
☐ Prickly Rose*, *Rosa acicularis*
☐ Prairie Rose*, *R. arkansana*
☐ Common Wild Rose*, *R. woodsii*
☐ Cultivated Rose+*^, *R sp.*
☐ Wild Red Raspberry*, *Rubus idaeus*
☐ Dewberry*^, *R. pubescens*
☐ European Mountain Ash+*, *Sorbus aucuparia*
☐ White Meadowsweet*, *Spiraea betulifolia*

PEA FAMILY, FABIACEAE
☐ Indian Milkvetch*, *Astragulus aboriginum*
☐ Cicer Milkvetch+*^, *A. cicer*
☐ Ground Plum, *A. crassicarpus*
☐ Purple Milkvetch*, *A. dasyglottis*
☐ Drummond's Milkvetch^, *A. drummondii*
☐ Elegant Milkvetch*, *A. eucosmos*
☐ Timber Milkvetch, *A. miser*
☐ Missouri Milkvetch, *A. missouriensis*
☐ Loose-flowered Milkvetch*^, *A. tenellus*
☐ Few-flowered Milkvetch, *A. vexilliflexus*
☐ Siberian Peashrub+*, *Caragana arborescens*
☐ Wild Licorice*, *Glycyrrhiza lepidota*
☐ Alpine Hedysarum*, *Hedysarum alpinum*
☐ Northern Hedysarum*, *H. boreale*
☐ Mackenzie's Hedysarum, *H. mackenzii*
☐ Cream-coloured Vetchling*, *Lathyrus ochroleucus*
☐ Perennial Lupine*, *Lupinus sericeus*
☐ Yellow Lucerne+, *Medicago falcata*
☐ Black Medick+*, *M. lupilina*
☐ Alfalfa+*, *M. sativa*

☐ White Sweet Clover+*, *Melilotus alba*
☐ Yellow Sweet Clover+*, *M. officinalis*
☐ Late Yellow Locoweed*, *Oxytropis monticola*
☐ Early Yellow Locoweed*, *O. sericea*
☐ Showy Locoweed*, *O. splendens*
☐ Viscid Locoweed*, *O. viscida*
☐ Purple Prairie Clover, *Petalostemon purpureum*
☐ Indian Bread Root*^, *Psorealea esculenta*
☐ Golden Bean*, *Thermopsis rhombifolia*
☐ Alsike Clover+, *Trifolium hybridum*
☐ Red Clover+*, *T. pratense*
☐ White Clover+*, *T. repens*
☐ Wild Vetch*, *Vicia americana*
☐ Tufted Vetch+*, *V. cracca*

GERANIUM FAMILY, GERANIACEAE
☐ Stork's-bill/Filaree+*^, *Erodium cicutarium*
☐ Sticky Purple Geranium*, *Geranium viscosissimum*

FLAX FAMILY, LINACEAE
☐ Wild Blue Flax*, *Linum lewisii*
☐ Yellow Flax, *L. rigidum*
☐ Common Flax+*^, *L. usitatissimum*

MILKWORT FAMILY, POLYGALACEAE
☐ Seneca Snakeroot*, *Polygala senega*

MAPLE FAMILY, ACERACEAE
☐ Manitoba Maple+*, *Acer negundo*

BUCKTHORN FAMILY, RHAMNACEAE
☐ European Buckthorn+*^, *Rhamnus cathartica*

VIOLET FAMILY, VIOLACEAE
☐ Early Blue Violet*, *Viola adunca*
☐ Western Canada White Violet*, *V. canadensis*
☐ Bog Violet*, *V. nephrophylla*
☐ Yellow Prairie Violet, *V. nuttallii*
☐ Marsh Violet, *V. palustris*
☐ Pansy, *V. tricolor*

OLEASTER FAMILY, ELEAGNACEAE
☐ Wolf Willow*, *Eleagnus commutata*
☐ Sea Buckthorn+*^, *Hippophae rhamnoides*
☐ Thorny Buffaloberry*, *Shepherdia argentea*
☐ Canada Buffaloberry*, *S. canadensis*

EVENING PRIMROSE FAMILY, ONAGRACEAE
☐ Common Fireweed*, *Epilobium angustifolium*
☐ Northern Willowherb*^, *E. ciliatum*
☐ Scarlet Butterflyweed*, *Gaura coccinea*
☐ Yellow Even.Primrose*, *Oenothera biennis*

WATER-MILFOIL FAMILY, HALORAGACEAE
☐ Water-Milfoil, *Myriophyllum exalbescens*

MARE'S-TAIL FAMILY, HIPPURIDACEAE
☐ Common Mare's-tail*, *Hippuris vulgaris*

GINSENG FAMILY, ARALIACEAE

☐ Wild Sarsaparilla*, *Aralia nudicaulis*

CARROT FAMILY, APIACEAE
☐ Water Hemlock, *Cicuta maculata*
☐ Cow Parsnip*, *Heracleum lanatum*
☐ White Prairie Parsley, *Lomatium macrocarpum*
☐ Rough-seeded Musineon, *Musineon divaricatum*
☐ Snakeroot*, *Sanicula marilandica*
☐ Heart-leaved Alexanders*, *Zizia aptera*

DOGWOOD FAMILY, CORNACEAE
☐ Red-osier Dogwood*, *Cornus stolonifera*

WINTERGREEN FAMILY, PYROLACEAE
☐ One-sided Wintergreen*, *Orthilia secunda*
☐ Pink Wintergreen*, *Pyrola asarifolia*

HEATH FAMILY, ERICACEAE
☐ Common Bearberry*, *Arctostaphyllos uva-ursi*

PRIMROSE FAMILY, PRIMULACEAE
☐ Fairy Candelabra, *Androsace septentrionalis*
☐ Mountain Shooting Star, *Dodecatheon conjugens*
☐ Saline Shooting Star*, *D. pulchellum*
☐ Mealy Primrose*, *Primula incana*

OLIVE FAMILY, OLEACEAE
☐ Green Ash+*^, *Fraxinus pensylvanica*
☐ Japanese Lilac+*^, *Syringa reticulata*
☐ Common Lilac+*, *S. vulgaris*

GENTIAN FAMILY, GENTIANACEAE
☐ Prairie Gentian, *Gentiana affinis*
☐ Northern Gentian, *Gentianella amarella*

DOGBANE FAMILY, APOCYNACEAE
☐ Spreading Dogbane*, *Apocynum androsaemilifolium*

MORNING-GLORY FAMILY, CONVOLVULACEAE
☐ Field Bindweed+*^, *Convolvulus arvensis*
☐ Hedge Bindweed+*^, *Convolvulus sepia*

PHLOX FAMILY, POLEMONACEAE
☐ Moss Phlox, *Phlox hoodii*

BORAGE FAMILY, BORAGINACEAE
☐ Viper's Bugloss+*^, *Echium vulgare*
☐ Large-flowered Stickseed*, *Hackelia floribunda*
☐ Bluebur+*, *Lappula squarrosa.*
☐ Narrow-leaved Puccoon, *Lithospermum incisum*
☐ Woolly Gromwell*, *L. ruderale*
☐ Tall Lungwort*, *Mertensia paniculata*
☐ Forget-me-not+*^, *Myosotis sp.*
☐ Western False Gromwell*^, *Onosmodium molle*

MINT FAMILY, LABIATAE
☐ Hemp-nettle+*, *Galeopsis tetrahit*
☐ Wild Mint*, *Mentha arvensis*
☐ Wild Bergamot*, *Monarda fistulosa*
☐ Hedge-nettle, *Stachys palustris*

FIGWORT FAMILY, SCROPHULARIACEAE

- ☐ Common Yellow Paintbrush*, *Castilleja lutescens*
- ☐ Eyebright*^, *Euphrasia arctica*
- ☐ Broad Leaved Toadflax+*^, *Linaria dalmatica*
- ☐ Butter-and-eggs+*, *L. vulgaris*
- ☐ Owl-clover, *Orthocarpus luteus*
- ☐ Elephant's-head*, *Pedicularis groenlandica*
- ☐ Smooth Blue Beard-tongue*, *Penstemon nitidus*
- ☐ Yellow Rattle*, *Rhinanthes minor*
- ☐ Common Mullein+*^, *Verbascum thapsus*
- ☐ Long-spike Speedwell+, *Veronica longifolia*
- ☐ Purselane Speedwell+*^, *V. peregrina*

BLADDERWORT FAMILY, LENTIBULARIACEAE

- ☐ Common Butterwort*, *Pinguicula vulgaris*

PLANTAIN FAMILY, PLANTAGINACEAE

- ☐ Common Plantain+*, *Plantago major*

MADDER FAMILY, RUBIACEAE

- ☐ Northern Bedstraw*, *Galium boreale*
- ☐ Sweet-scented Bedstraw, *G. triflorum*
- ☐ Yellow Bedstraw+, *G. verum*

HONEYSUCKLE FAMILY, CAPRIFOLIACEAE

- ☐ Twining Honeysuckle*, *Lonicera dioica*
- ☐ Bracted Honeysuckle, *L. involucrata*
- ☐ Tartarian Honeysuckle+*, *L. tatarica*
- ☐ BlackElderberry+, *Sambucus racemosa var. melanocarpa*
- ☐ Cut-leaved Elderberry+, *S. r. laciniata*
- ☐ Red Elderberry+*, *S. r. pubens*
- ☐ Snowberry*, *Symphoricarpos albus*
- ☐ Buckbrush*, *S. occidentalis*
- ☐ Squashberry*, *Viburnum edule*
- ☐ Wayfaring Bush+*^, *V. lantana*
- ☐ Cranberry Viburnum*^, *V. trilobum*

BLUEBELL FAMILY, CAMPANULACEAE

- ☐ Creeping Bellflower+*, *Campanula rapunculoides*
- ☐ Harebell*, *C. rotundifolia*

COMPOSITE/DAISY FAMILY, COMPOSITAE

- ☐ Common Yarrow*, *Achillea millefolium* (includes a pale pink form)
- ☐ False Dandelion, *Agoseris glauca*
- ☐ Small Everlasting, *Antennaria nitida*
- ☐ Small-flowered Everlasting, *A. parviflora*
- ☐ Showy Everlasting, *A. pulcherrima*
- ☐ Yellow Chamomile+, *Anthemis tinctoria*
- ☐ Common Burdock+*, *Arctium minus*
- ☐ Heart-leaved Arnica, *Arnica cordifolia*
- ☐ Shining Arnica, *A. fulgens*
- ☐ Spear-leaved Arnica, *A. lonchophylla*
- ☐ Absinthe Wormwood+*, *Artemisia absinthium*
- ☐ Biennial Sagewort, *A. biennis*
- ☐ Plains Sagewort, *A. campestris*
- ☐ Dragonwort+*^, *A. dracunculus*

- ☐ Pasture Sagewort*, *A. frigida*
- ☐ Prairie Sagewort*, *A. ludoviciana*
- ☐ Alpine Aster, *Aster alpinus*
- ☐ Canescent Aster, *A. canescens*
- ☐ Lindley's Aster, *A. ciliolatus*
- ☐ Showy Aster*, *A. conspicuus*
- ☐ Tufted White Prairie Aster, *A. ericoides*
- ☐ Creeping White Prairie Aster, *A. falcatus*
- ☐ Western Willow Aster, *A. hesperius*
- ☐ Smooth Blue Aster*, *A. laevis*
- ☐ Arctic Aster*^, *A. sibericus*
- ☐ Safflower+, *Carthamus tinctorius*
- ☐ Diffuse Knapweed, *Centaurea diffusa*
- ☐ Ox-eye Daisy+*^, *Chrysanthemum leucanthemum*
- ☐ Canada Thistle+*, *Cirsium arvense*
- ☐ Wavy-leaved Thistle, *C. undulatum*
- ☐ Canada Horseweed, *Conyza canadensis*
- ☐ Annual Hawk's-beard+*^, *Crepis tectorum*
- ☐ Globe Thistle+, *Echinops sphaerocephalus*
- ☐ Tufted Fleabane, *Erigeron caespitosus*
- ☐ Smooth Fleabane*, *E. glabellus*
- ☐ Philadelphia Fleabane, *E. philadelphicus*
- ☐ Gumweed, *Grindelia squarrosa*
- ☐ Spinulose Ironplant, *Haplopappus spinulosus*
- ☐ Rhombic-leaved Sunflower, *Helianthus subrhomboides*
- ☐ Golden Aster, *Heterotheca villosa*
- ☐ Narrow-leaved Hawkweed*, *Hieraceum umbellatum*
- ☐ Gaillardia*, *Gaillardia aristata*
- ☐ Common Blue Lettuce*, *Lactuca pulchella*
- ☐ Prickly Lettuce+, *L. serriola*
- ☐ Pineappleweed+*, *Matricaria matricarioides*
- ☐ Scentless Chamomile+*, *M. perforata*
- ☐ Wild Chamomile+, *M. recutita*
- ☐ Silvery Groundsel, *Senecio canus*
- ☐ Balsam Groundsel*, *S. pauperculus*
- ☐ Thin-leaved Ragwort, *S. pseudaureus*
- ☐ Common Groundsel+, *S. vulgaris*
- ☐ Canada Goldenrod, *Solidago canadensis*
- ☐ Late Goldenrod*, *S. gigantea*
- ☐ Flat-topped Goldenrod*^, *S. graminifolia*
- ☐ Low Goldenrod*, *S. missouriensis*
- ☐ Showy Goldenrod, *S. nemoralis*
- ☐ Stiff Goldenrod, *S. rigida*
- ☐ Prickly Annual Sowthistle+, *Sonchus asper*
- ☐ Perennial Sowthistle*, *S. uliginosus*
- ☐ Common Tansy+*, *Tanacetum vulgare*
- ☐ Red-seeded Dandelion+, *Taraxacum laevigatum*
- ☐ Common Dandelion+*, *T. officinale*
- ☐ Common Goat's-beard+*, *Tragopodium dubius*
- ☐ Meadow Goat's-beard+*^, *T. pratense*

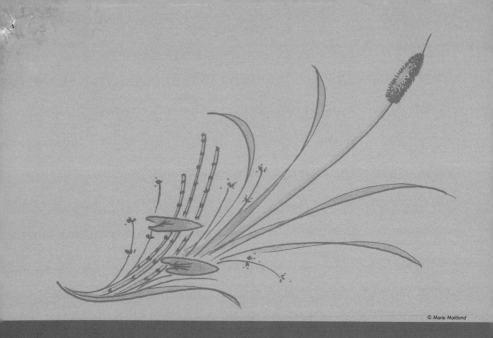

© Marie Maitland

APPENDIX TWO

CHECKLIST OF BIRDS OF EDWORTHY PARK AND VICINITY

By Reid Barclay, 2002

LEGEND: X = KNOWN TO HAVE BRED IN PARK   ? = PERHAPS BREEDS IN PARK – QUESTIONABLE

SPECIES:	BREEDS	OCCURRENCE:
Common Loon		Rare spring/fall migrant
Horned Grebe		Rare spring/fall migrant
Red-necked Grebe		Rare spring/fall migrant
Eared Grebe		Rare spring/fall migrant
American White Pelican		Occasional summer visitor
Double-crested Cormorant		Occasional summer visitor
Great Blue Heron		Uncommon spring/fall migrant
Black-crowned Night-heron		Rare migrant (fall)
Sandhill Crane		Accidental
Tundra Swan		Rare spring/fall migrant
Canada Goose	X	Common spring/summer/fall rare winter
Wood Duck		Occasional summer visitor
Green-winged Teal		Occasional spring/fall migrant
Mallard	X	Common resident year-round
Northern Pintail		Rare spring/fall migrant
Blue-winged Teal		Uncommon spring/fall migrant
Cinnamon Teal		Rare spring/fall migrant
Northern Shoveler		Rare spring/fall migrant
Gadwall		Uncommon spring/fall migrant
American Wigeon		Uncommon spring/fall migrant
Lesser Scaup		Uncommon spring/fall migrant
Harlequin Duck		Rare migrant
White-winged Scoter		Rare migrant
Common Goldeneye	X	Uncommon resident
Bufflehead		Uncommon spring/fall migrant
Hooded Merganser		Uncommon spring/fall migrant
Common Merganser	X(?)	Common summer/uncommon winter
Red-breasted Merganser		Rare migrant
Osprey		Uncommon summer visitor
Bald Eagle		Uncommon fall/winter visitor
Northern Harrier		Rare migrant
Sharp-shinned Hawk		Uncommon migrant
Cooper's Hawk	X	Uncommon migrant
Northern Goshawk		Rare winter visitor
Broad-winged Hawk		Very rare migrant
Swainson's Hawk	X	Common migrant/uncommon summer
Red-tailed Hawk	X	Common migrant/common summer
Rough-legged Hawk		Uncommon spring/fall migrant
Golden Eagle		Rare migrant
American Kestrel	X	Uncommon summer resident
Merlin	X	Uncommon year round resident
Peregrine Falcon		Very rare migrant
Prairie Falcon		Very rare migrant

Gray Partridge	X	Uncommon resident
Ring-necked Pheasant	X	Uncommon resident
Sora	X	Uncommon summer resident
American Coot		Uncommon migrant
Semipalmated Plover		Very rare migrant
Piping Plover		Accidental
Killdeer	X	Common summer resident
Greater Yellowlegs		Uncommon spring/fall migrant
Lesser Yellowlegs		Uncommon spring/fall migrant
Solitary Sandpiper		Uncommon spring/fall migrant
Spotted Sandpiper	X	Common summer resident
Semipalmated Sandpiper		Rare fall migrant
Baird's Sandpiper		Rare fall migrant
Common Snipe	X	Uncommon summer resident
Franklin's Gull		Common summer visitor
Mew Gull		Very rare fall migrant
Ring-billed Gull		Common summer resident
California Gull		Common summer resident
Herring Gull		Uncommon spring/fall migrant
Thayer's Gull		Rare spring/fall migrant
Common Tern		Rare spring/fall migrant
Rock Dove	X	Common resident
Mourning Dove	X	Rare summer resident
Great Horned Owl	X	Uncommon year round resident
Northern Pygmy-Owl		Very rare (2 records)
Barred Owl		Very rare (1 record)
Northern Saw-whet Owl	?	Very rare
Common Night Hawk		Rare migrant
Ruby throated Hummingbird	?	Rare migrant/uncommon summer resident
Calliope Hummingbird		Very rare migrant
Rufous Hummingbird	?	Uncommon migrant/uncommon summer resident
Belted Kingfisher	X	Uncommon summer resident
Lewis' Woodpecker		Very rare migrant (3 records)
Yellow-bellied Sapsucker	?	Uncommon migrant
Red-naped Sapsucker	?	Uncommon migrant
Downy Woodpecker	X	Common resident
Hairy Woodpecker	X	Uncommon resident
Three-toed Woodpecker		Rare winter visitor
Northern Flicker	X	Common summer/rare winter
Pileated Woodpecker		Rare migrant
Black-backed Woodpecker		Rare winter visitor
Olive-sided Flycatcher		Uncommon spring/fall migrant
Western Wood-Pewee	X	Common summer resident
Alder Flycatcher		Rare migrant
Least Flycatcher	X	Common summer resident
Dusky Flycatcher		Rare migrant-fall
"Western" Flycatcher		Rare migrant
Eastern Phoebe	X	Uncommon summer

Species		Status
Say's Phoebe		Rare spring/fall
Western Kingbird		Rare migrant
Eastern Kingbird	X	Common summer resident
Tree Swallow	X	Common summer resident
Northern Rough-winged Swallow	X	Uncommon summer resident
Bank Swallow	X	Uncommon summer resident
Cliff Swallow	X	Common summer resident
Barn Swallow	X	Uncommon summer resident
Blue Jay	X	Uncommon year round resident
Black-billed Magpie	X	Common resident
American Crow	X	Common summer resident (abundant)
Common Raven		Year round resident
Black-capped Chickadee	X	Common resident
Mountain Chickadee		Rare – winter
Boreal Chickadee		Rare/uncommon winter
Chestnut-backed Chickadee		Accidental
Red-breasted Nuthatch	X	Common resident
White-breasted Nuthatch	X	Common resident
Brown Creeper	?	Uncommon – winter
House Wren	X	Common summer resident
Marsh Wren		Rare migrant
Golden-crowned Kinglet		Uncommon winter resident
Ruby-crowned Kinglet	X	Common summer resident
Townsend's Solitaire		Rare migrant
Veery	X	Uncommon summer resident
Swainson's Thrush		Common migrant
Hermit Thrush		Uncommon migrant
Gray-cheeked Thrush		Uncommon migrant
American Robin	X	Common summer/winter uncommon
Gray Catbird	X	Uncommon summer resident
Brown Thrasher	X	Uncommon summer resident
American Pipit		Uncommon migrant
Bohemian Waxwing		Common winter resident
Cedar Waxwing	X	Common summer resident
European Starling	X	Common resident
Blue-headed Vireo		Uncommon migrant
Warbling Vireo	X	Common summer resident
Philadelphia Vireo		Rare migrant
Red-eyed Vireo	X	Uncommon summer resident
Tennessee Warbler		Uncommon summer resident/common migrant
Orange-crowned Warbler		Uncommon summer resident/common migrant
Yellow Warbler	X	Abundant summer resident/common migrant
Chestnut-sided Warbler		Rare migrant-fall
Magnolia Warbler		Rare migrant – fall
Cape May Warbler		Rare migrant – fall
Yellow-rumped Warbler		Common migrant – spring, fall
Townsend's Warbler		Uncommon migrant
Black-throated Green Warbler		Rare migrant

Species		Status
Blackburnian Warbler		Rare migrant
Palm Warbler		Rare migrant
Bay-breasted Warbler		Rare migrant
Blackpoll Warbler		Uncommon migrant
Black-and-white Warbler		Rare migrant
American Redstart		Uncommon migrant
Ovenbird		Uncommon migrant
Northern Waterthrush		Uncommon migrant
Connecticut Warbler		Rare migrant
Mourning Warbler		Rare migrant
MacGillivray's Warbler	X	Uncommon summer resident
Common Yellowthroat	X	Common summer resident
Wilson's Warbler		Common migrant
Canada Warbler		Rare migrant
Western Tanager	(?)	Uncommon summer resident/migrant
Rose-breasted Grosbeak	(?)	Uncommon summer resident/migrant
Black-headed Grosbeak		Rare migrant
Lazuli Bunting		Rare migrant
Spotted Towhee	X	Uncommon summer resident
American Tree Sparrow		Uncommon winter resident/migrant
Chipping Sparrow	X	Common summer resident
Clay-coloured Sparrow	X	Common summer resident
Savannah Sparrow	X	Common summer resident
Grasshopper Sparrow		Rare migrant
LeConte's Sparrow		Rare migrant
Song Sparrow	X	Common summer resident
Lincoln's Sparrow	X	Uncommon summer resident
Swamp Sparrow		Rare migrant
White-throated Sparrow	X	Common summer resident
White-crowned Sparrow		Common migrant
Dark-eyed Junco	X	Uncommon resident
Red winged Blackbird	X	Common summer resident
Western Meadowlark	X	Rare migrant – used to breed
Rusty Blackbird		Rare migrant
Brewer's Blackbird	(?)	Uncommon summer resident/migrant
Common Grackle	X	Uncommon summer resident
Brown-headed Cowbird	X	Common summer resident
Northern Oriole	X	Common summer resident
Pine Grosbeak		Uncommon winter resident
Purple Finch		Rare summer resident/migrant
Red Crossbill		Uncommon winter resident
White-winged Crossbill	X	Variable occurrence
Common Redpoll		Common winter resident
Pine Siskin	X	Common summer resident
American Goldfinch	X	Common summer resident
Evening Grosbeak		Rare migrant
House Sparrow	(?)	Common resident

© Marie Maitland

CONTRIBUTORS

CONTRIBUTORS

TEXT AND ARTWORK

REID BARCLAY has been a field naturalist for over thirty years and undertakes environmental assessment studies, including studies of bird populations. He has been involved in working at the community level to preserve significant natural areas from development

RON LINDEN grew up in Calgary and has a keen interest in local history. With a grant received from the Alberta Historical Resources Foundation, he researched and wrote a history of Lawrey Gardens.

MARIE MAITLAND, born in Calgary, is a graduate of design and has been illustrating since 1983. Working from her West Hillhurst studio, she is an active community volunteer, fanatical gardener and also spends countless hours at Lawrey Gardens.

DR. JERRY OSBORN is a Professor of Geology in the Dept. of Geology and Geophysics at the University of Calgary; his research specialties are Quaternary, surficial, and urban geology.

KATE PEACH is a professional archaeologist and currently works for FMA Heritage Resources Consultants, Inc. She has worked in the field in Manitoba, Saskatchewan, Alberta, Ontario, Idaho, and Crimea. She has worked on collections from these areas as well as from the Canadian Arctic and Tunisia.

DR. TED PIKE has taught high school science for several years. He has published extensively on fossil insects preserved in Cretaceous amber. He is one of the co-authors of *Alberta Butterflies* and with Myrna Pearman co-authored *Alberta Nature Scape*.

GEORGE WILSON was born and raised in Ottawa. A Calgarian since 1959, he is a retired geologist who enjoys hiking and photography.

CRAIG SCOTT is a Ph.D. student in the Laboratory of Vertebrate Palaeontology in the Dept. of Biological Sciences at the University of Alberta.

MICHELLE THEAM is a biology student at the University of Calgary with a lifelong interest in painting and sketching.

MONICA WEBSTER has ten years of field experience in archaeology, including work in Alberta, Saskatchewan, Mexico and Africa. She currently works with FMA Heritage Resources Inc.

GUSTAVE J. YAKI has led groups on nature tours around the world for the past 35 years and has a keen interest in, and encyclopaedic knowledge of, birds and wildflowers. He is a member of the Calgary Field Naturalists' Society and leads nature walks.

PHOTOGRAPHY

DR. WAYNE LYNCH left a career as an emergency medicine physician in 1979 to pursue a full-time career as a professional wildlife photographer and science writer. He is Canada's best known nature photographer and has published more than a dozen natural history books including *Married to the Wind: A Study of the Prairie Grasslands*, *Wild Birds Across The Prairies*, and *The Great Northern Forest*.

DR. OSWALD F. WACHTLER obtained an M.D. degree from the University of Vienna and has resided in Calgary for many years where he currently practices family medicine. His extensive travels have led him, among other places, to Bhutan, Tibet, India, the Himalayas, Galapagos, Antarctica, South America, Africa and Asia.

MICHAEL BUCKLEY, one of the winners of the Edworthy Park Heritage Society's 2001 photo contest, pursues his love for wildflower and bird photography and is the owner of Blue Pond Studios (www.bluepondstudios.com). He and his wife Alisa may often be found in Southern Alberta capturing the perfect photo.

L. McCONNELL has a keen interest in butterflies. When not busy with her family, her favourite pastime is "sitting on a bench on the Douglas Fir Trail watching life and butterflies go by". She is also an accomplished amateur pianist.

E. GILLIAM is a retired fourth generation Calgarian who dabbles in bird photography and is interested in local history and gardening. He is particularly fond of the upper portion of the Douglas Fir Trail with its abundance of migratory warblers to photograph.

M. BAILEY grew up in Calgary and has focussed on the preservation of rough fescue prairie and other natural habitats. She has a great love for collies, horses, and nature. She is an accomplished artist specializing in oil painting and sculptures.

PAUL BEAULIEU, another winner of the Edworthy Park Heritage Society's photo contest, pursues his interest in photography by focussing on nature and street photography. Originally from Montreal, he has lived in Calgary for several years. He currently works in Calgary as a software developer.

SEAN JACKSON grew up in Wildwood, adjacent to Edworthy Park. He is also a winner of the Edworthy Park Heritage Society's photo contest. He is the father of two young children.

ANTHONY HEAZELL is originally from the Cambridge area of England. He now lives in Calgary and is a keen birder and photographer.

URS KALLEN enjoys spending time in the outdoors, mountain climbing, hiking and photography. He is co-owner of Kallen Graphics Ltd., an award-winning printing company in Calgary.

KATHLEEN ROMAN was born and raised in Alberta and has lived in Calgary for several years. A keen birder and bird photographer, Kathleen is a long-time member of the Calgary Field Naturalists' Society.

GILLEAN DAFFERN enjoys hiking, scrambling and wildflower photographing. She is a co-owner of Rocky Mountain Books, a Calgary publishing company, and is best-known for the very popular *Kananaskis Country Trail Guide*.

DAVE ELPHINSTONE is a well-known naturalist and the Natural Areas Management Co-ordinator for the City of Calgary. He wrote *Inglewood Bird Sanctuary A Place for All Seasons*.

LINDSAY UTTING, a teacher, enjoys walking along the Douglas Fir Trail. She is on the Board of Directors of the Calgary Rock and Alpine Garden Society.

© Marie Maitland

FURTHER READING

GEOLOGY

Jackson, L.E., and Wilson, M.C. editors, 1987: *Geology of the Calgary Area*, Canadian Society of Petroleum Geologists, 148 pp.

Osborn, Gerald and Rajewicz, Rene. 1988: "Urban Geology of Calgary", *Urban Geology of Canadian Cities*, edited by O. White and P. Karrow, Geological Association of Canada Special Publication 42, pp. 93-115.

Poulton, T., Neumar, T., Osborn, G., Edwards, D. and Wozniak, P. 2002: *Geoscape Calgary* (poster), Geological Survey of Canada Miscellaneous Report 72.

PALAEONTOLOGY

Scott, Craig S. 2001: *Palaeontological Resources Impact Assessment for the City of Calgary*. City of Calgary, 16 pp.

Stewart, Wilson N. and Rothwell, Gar W. 1983, 1993: *Paleobotany and the evolution of plants*. Cambridge University Press, Cambridge, England. 521 pp.

[a comprehensive text for university students in the evolution of plants through fossils]

ARCHAEOLOGY

Wilson, Michael C. *Once Upon a River: Archaeology and Geology of the Bow River Valley at Calgary, Alberta, Canada*. Archaeological Survey of Canada, Paper No. 114, National Museum of Man Mercury Series, 465 pp.

[definitive work explaining the archaeology and geology of the area]

PLANTS

Brown, Annora. *Old Man's Garden*. (Originally published 1954, Toronto: J.M. Dent & Sons), republished 2000: Algrove Publishing Limited, Ottawa, 268 pp.

[a very reasonably priced reprint of a classic by Alberta artist and author Annora Brown with charming woodcuts and available at Lee Valley Tools Ltd. stores]

Bush, C. Dana. 1990: *The Compact Guide to Wildflowers of the Rockies*. Lone Pine Publishing, Edmonton, Alberta, 142 pp.

[superbly illustrated pocket-sized guide with intriguing facts about wildflowers]

Cormack, R.G.H. 1967: *Wild Flowers of Alberta*.* Government of Alberta, Department of Industry and Development. Queen's Printer, Alberta, 415 pp.

*[Very informative classic about Alberta wildflowers]**

Johnston, Derek, Kershaw, L., MacKinnon, A., Pojar, J. 1995: *Plants of the Western Boreal Forest & Aspen Parkland*. Lone Pine Publishing, Edmonton, Alberta, 392 pp.

Budd, A.C. 1994: (Revised and Enlarged by J. Looman and K.F. Best) *Budd's Flora of the Canadian Prairie Provinces*. Agriculture Canada Publication 1662, 863 pp.

[well-organized and comprehensive botany/flora book – key to identifying flowers in the field]

Scotter, George W., and Flygare, Hälle. 1986: first printing. *Wildflowers of the Canadian Rockies*. Alpine Book Peddlers, Canmore, Alberta, 170 pp.

[exquisite photographs and concise, interesting text]

Vance, F.R., Jowsey, J.R., McLean, J.S., Switzer, F.A. 1999: *Wildflowers across the Prairies*. Greystone Books, Douglas and McIntyre Publishing Group, 383 pp.

[still one of the definitive works on prairie wildflowers. A reprint of a classic with an added, highly informative and useful section on grasses]

Wilkinson, Kathleen. 1990: *Trees and Shrubs of Alberta*. Lone Pine Publishing, Edmonton, Alberta, 191 pp.

[comprehensive book with high quality photographs]

Wilkinson, Kathleen. 1999: *Wildflowers of Alberta*. Lone Pine Publishing, Edmonton, Alberta, 364 pp.

[thorough guide to Alberta wildflowers with beautiful photographs]

BUTTERFLIES

Acorn, J.H. 1993: *Butterflies of Alberta*. Lone Pine Publishers, Edmonton, Alberta, 143 pp.

[a handy book which covers the basics and provides an excellent overview of Alberta butterflies for the layperson]

Bird, C.D., Hilchie, G.J., Kondla, N.G., Pike, E.M. and Sperling, F.A.H. 1995: *Alberta Butterflies*. The Provincial Museum of Alberta, Edmonton, 349 pp.

[the definitive scientific work on all of the species of Alberta butterflies, including descriptions of their habitats, larval and adult food and ranges – a must-have for the serious butterfly aficionado.]

Feltwell, Dr. John. 1986: *The Natural History of Butterflies*. * Facts on File, Inc. New York, 133 pp.

[superb book by one of Britain's leading butterfly experts and conservationists - Dr. Feltwell has written many books on butterflies around the world]

Layberry, R.A., Hall, P.W. and Lafontaine, J.D. 1998. *The Butterflies of Canada*. University of Toronto Press, Toronto, Ontario. 280 pp.

BIRDS

Lynch, Wayne. 1999: *Wild Birds Across the Prairies.* Fifth House Ltd., Calgary, Alberta, 138 pp.

[exquisite photos, captivating text.]

Semenchuk, Glen P., editor. 1992: *The Atlas of Breeding Birds of Alberta.* Federation of Alberta Naturalists. Edmonton, Alberta. 391 pp.

[a must-have for Alberta birders]

AMPHIBIANS AND REPTILES

Russell, Anthony P. and Bauer, Aaron M. 2000: *The Amphibians and Reptiles of Alberta. A Field Guide and Primer of Boreal Herpetology.* Second Edition. University of Calgary Press. 279 pp.

[the definitive work on amphibians and reptiles in Alberta with colour photographs by Dr. Wayne Lynch]

NATURAL HISTORY

Gayton, Don. 1990, 1992: *The Wheatgrass Mechanism. Science and Imagination in the Western Canadian Landscape.* Fifth House Publishers, 156 pp.

[captures the soul, the essence of the prairies in relation to science]

Hallworth, Beryl. editor, 1988: *Nose Hill: A Popular Guide.** Calagary Field Naturalists' Society, Calgary, Alberta. 133 pp. plus colour plates.

[fact-filled book covering geology, archaeology, history, habitats, plants, birds and mammals of Nose Hill – much of the information is relevant to Edworthy Park and other natural areas of Calgary]

Lynch, Wayne Dr. 2001: *The Great Northern Kingdom. Life in the Boreal Forest.* Fitzhenry & Whiteside Limited, Markham, Ontario. 160 pp.

[exquisite photos and interesting text by Canada's best-known professional nature photographer – Dr. Wayne Lynch's many books on various topics are all of the same high calibre]

Sherrington, Peter, editor. 1975: *Calgary's Natural Areas. A Popular Guide.** Calgary Field Naturalists' Society, Calgary, Alberta. 184 pp.

[superb guide to Calgary's natural areas – a timeless classic!]

Willock, Thomas. 1990: *A Prairie Coulee.** Lone Pine Publishing, Edmonton, Alberta. 95 pp.

[captures the essence of the prairie coulee, its flora and fauna – excellent photos]

ETHNOBOTANY

Thomson, William A.R., M.D., editor. 1978: *Medicines from the Earth.** McGraw-Hill Book Company (U.K.) Limited, Maidenhead, England. 207 pp.

[a comprehensive book on the medicinal use of plants with contributions by well-known ethnobotanists including Richard Schultes, and others]

HISTORY

Clayton, Jill. August, 1990: *Brickburn Part of Calgary's Heritage.* Unpublished, Calgary Parks and Recreation. 52 pp. plus photos.

[well-researched manuscript based on primary sources and interviews with many people who had first-hand knowledge of Brickburn]

Edworthy Park Heritage Society. 1991, reprinted 1994: *Early Days in Edworthy Park and the Neighboring Areas of Brickburn and Lawrey Gardens.** Calgary, Alberta, 31 pp.

Linden, Ron. 1992. *Lawrey Gardens.* Unpublished manuscript.

[well-researched manuscript on the history of Lawrey Gardens, from primary sources]

MacEwen, Grant. 1975 (second edition): *Calgary Cavalcade.** Western Producer Book Service, Saskatoon, 200 pp.

Manson, Jack M. 1982: *Bricks in Alberta.** Published by John M. Manson, Edmonton, Alberta, 154 pp.

[canvasses the historic brick plants in Alberta, detailing how the bricks were made and unique facts about brick operations – a piece of Alberta history!]

MISCELLANEOUS

Onions, C.T., editor. 1966: *Oxford Dictionary of English Etymology.* Oxford University Press, Oxford, England. 1024 pp.

[key book on etymology of English words – also available as the Oxford Concise Dictionary of Etymology]

* Out of print but may be available at libraries and second-hand bookstores.

INDEX OF PHOTOS